EDUCATING
THE SUB-NORMAL CHILD

EDUCATING THE SUB-NORMAL CHILD

Aspects of the work of a Junior School for Educationally Sub-normal Children

by
FRANCES LLOYD
(DIPLOMA IN THE TEACHING OF E.S.N. CHILDREN)

WITH A FOREWORD BY
M. F. CLEUGH

PHILOSOPHICAL LIBRARY
NEW YORK

*Published 1953 by the Philosophical Library Inc.
15 East 40th Street, New York 16, N.Y.*

ALL RIGHTS RESERVED

PRINTED IN GREAT BRITAIN FOR PHILOSOPHICAL LIBRARY
BY JARROLD AND SONS LIMITED, NORWICH

FOREWORD

Many people, when reading books such as this, try to visualize the unknown school whose work is described. Usually it is imagined as a palace of modern comfort, generously staffed and equipped. The reader is then enabled to dismiss the more challenging suggestions by thinking, "It's all very well for her to talk, but it wouldn't work here under our conditions." So it may be useful to state plainly that the school of which Miss Lloyd is Head has many difficulties to overcome—an inconvenient and ugly building, the usual shortage of teachers, noise, dirt, and lack of amenities and equipment. It is, in fact, an 'ordinary' school and not a show school of the type to which authorities like to direct visitors.

The only thing that is not ordinary about it is the spirit that animates it—and I imagine that it is in the hope that this spirit can become more general that Miss Lloyd has written her book. Many of us, having read this book, will share that hope.

M. F. CLEUGH

CONTENTS

CHAPTER	PAGE
FOREWORD	v
INTRODUCTION	1
I SHOULD WE ATTEMPT TO EDUCATE THE MENTALLY HANDICAPPED?	5
II THE DEVELOPMENT OF MENTALLY HANDICAPPED CHILDREN AND THE CRITERION BY WHICH THEY SHOULD BE SELECTED FOR SPECIAL SCHOOL TREATMENT	12
III SOCIAL BACKGROUND AND PARENTS' ATTITUDES	18
PARENT-TEACHER ASSOCIATIONS	31
IV DELINQUENCY AMONG E.S.N. CHILDREN	33
V SOCIAL TRAINING IN THE SPECIAL SCHOOL	47
VI MISFITS IN THE SPECIAL E.S.N. SCHOOL	66
CASE STUDIES: RONALD	83
FRED BROWN	97
TONY GREEN	103
EXAMPLES OF EXPRESSION WORK	facing 92, 100
VII ACTIVITIES IN THE SPECIAL E.S.N. SCHOOL	110
CREATIVE ACTIVITY	112
LANGUAGE AND READING	118
NUMBER	128
A READING AND NUMBER ACTIVITY	135
AN ACTIVITY BASED ON SCHOOL MILK	136
VIII WHAT IS 'SUCCESS' IN SPECIAL SCHOOL TREATMENT?	140
INDEX	145

INTRODUCTION
THE SPECIAL SCHOOL FOR EDUCATIONALLY SUB-NORMAL CHILDREN

Every society has to decide how to deal with the handicapped. The solutions offered by different societies have been very varied, both in their methods and in their success. As teachers we are concerned rather with the problem as it affects children and adolescents, especially in regard to their education. There are people who think that to attempt to educate the mentally handicapped is absurd. Others think that such children are capable of receiving education in ordinary schools, provided that special provision is made for them there. Many Local Education Authorities appear to subscribe to this view, while others provide special schools for all types of handicapped children, the blind, the deaf, the delicate, the physically handicapped, the maladjusted, and the educationally sub-normal. These last are sent to special schools only if their intelligence quotient falls below 70 or 75. Above this, they are supposed to receive special educational treatment in ordinary schools. If the I.Q. falls below 50 they are usually deemed ineducable, and receive training in an occupation centre.

Those of us who are privileged to work in schools for the mentally handicapped, have a burning conviction that such children are well worth the care and patience expended in educating them, and most of us also feel that the prepared environment of a special school is the most suitable for their development. Away from competition, in security and peace, they can gradually work out their salvation. In the special school the child finds that he is acceptable, and that the little contribution he can make, perhaps only a willingness to co-operate, is acceptable too. He does what he can. No more is asked of him. No longer is he judged by the criterion of innate ability. He need not succeed in the basic subjects in order to escape failure. He is valued as a personality, rather than as a reader or writer or arithmetician. The development of each child is very carefully watched, and what he needs is put before him at each moment, so that his personality and his abilities are fed and strengthened. Our very small classes make this concentration on the needs and development of each child possible, and the child is enabled to progress slowly, sometimes indeed almost imperceptibly, at his own pace, peacefully and without any hustling.

Yet there are people who still feel that there is a stigma attached to a special school for the mentally handicapped, even though they do not appear to attach any such stigma to schools for the blind, for example, or for delicate children. We hear no talk of the wrong we are doing in segregating these blind or delicate children in a school where their handicap may to some extent be minimized. Why then, grudge a specially prepared environment to the educationally sub-normal child, and talk of 'stigma'? This prejudice can be understood when it crops up among ignorant people, but unfortunately it can also be found among people who should be better informed. There is a recent book, written by a teacher, where the old prejudice is given a new impetus in the following passage: 'Children found to have a low intelligence quotient are sent to special schools, colloquially known as (1) "silly schools". These children, however, are trained, so that when they leave school they can take their place in society. (2) This being the objective of the special schools, it would be better for those children of low I.Q. who (3) show no behaviour problems, (4) to remain in the normal school. They should, however, be relegated to a class for special methods of tuition. (5) Only children who cannot fit in with the games and social life of the school should be segregated.'

I hope, in the chapters which follow, to be able to establish that this author is describing exactly what a special school is *not*. (1) It is not a 'silly school'. The developing personalities described in some of the case studies should be sufficient to belie that very cruel nickname, but if those fail to convince, we have a collection of original paintings and other art work done in our school, which could never have come from the minds of 'silly' children. It is those who apply such names and perpetuate their use who create a stigma. What would be said of such cruel nicknames if the blind, and not the mentally handicapped children, were being held up to ridicule? (2) The E.S.N. school is not a training centre. The writer is obviously confusing its objective with that of the occupation centre. Of course the special school hopes to be able to train mentally handicapped children to take their place in society, but that is also included in the aims of an ordinary school. (3) The special school is not intended as a dumping-ground for troublesome children. Children should be recommended, not for their nuisance value, but because, by reason of low intelligence, they are unable to profit from the type of education provided in an ordinary school. It seems that, in the passage quoted, the E.S.N. school is being confused not only with the occupation centre, but also with the special schools for the maladjusted. (5) The writer is employing a social criterion for ascertainment at an age when an educational one is more appropriate, for he advocates that the socially able child should be left in an ordinary school without regard to his low intelligence. (4) I think that most of us who have had experience in both types of school would agree that it is calamitous for children to be kept in ordinary schools unless their intelligence warrants it. I would like to point out, too, that special methods of tuition are not enough. The whole atmosphere of the school and the attitude of the teacher must be specially fitted to the mentally handicapped child. There is a different orientation which is essential to the growth of these children, and special methods of tuition are no adequate substitute for all that the special school can offer.

In this book, then, I have attempted to discuss the educability of mentally handicapped children, the aims of the special school and how it can best achieve these aims, the social training of E.S.N. children with special reference to their own cultural background and their parents' attitudes, and how the mentally handicapped child who also appears emotionally disturbed can be helped through creative work to achieve adjustment. Although some examples have been drawn from the older E.S.N. girls (11–16) with whom I worked for six years, the emphasis throughout is on the work of the Junior E.S.N. School, where the foundations of the whole work are laid.

Chapter I

SHOULD WE ATTEMPT TO EDUCATE THE MENTALLY HANDICAPPED?

I have very often heard the opinion expressed that to educate mentally handicapped children with I.Q's between 50 and 75 is a waste of time, money and effort. On a superficial level this attitude may appear justified. Nevertheless I believe that such a conclusion is based either upon false values, or upon an uncritical acceptance of the jargon of cheap 'modernists'.

Our western civilization has been built upon a deep appreciation of the value of the human personality. Modernistic 'thinkers', in losing their reverence for the human personality, and in attempting to evaluate human beings upon their apparent degree of usefulness to the State, are threatening our whole civilization. Many deplore the fact that money and skill are 'wasted' upon those who can only be a burden to the State. Some advocate sterilization, euthanasia or other means of extermination for those whom they are pleased to regard as useless. 'What a society we could build,' they say, 'if the money, time and effort now expended upon the mentally handicapped, the incurables, the aged, and the insane, were used to provide more and more benefits for the normal and supernormal!' From a purely material standpoint they may appear to have a case, but when their policy is put into action, what sort of a State do they build, and what becomes of it? We have only to look at Sparta in the ancient world, and Nazi Germany in our own times, to find the answer. The so-called 'useless' were liquidated, but where is the superman now, and where his super-State? It seems to be necessary for the health and balance of society that the strong should care for the weak, and the fortunate for the unfortunate. In fact, the well-being of the

State depends upon its maintaining a true sense of values, and upon its being able to integrate its many components on a basis of love, compassion and self-sacrifice, expressed in terms of a true reverence for the unique value of each individual.

However, I imagine that even the most thorough-going 'modernist' would hesitate to liquidate all those whose intelligence quotient falls below 70 or 75. Yet, if they think it wasteful to educate them, what alternatives can they offer?

Would they leave them in their homes, without education? Many of their homes are poverty stricken, many are careless and inadequate, some have low moral standards. If unstable children are left to grow up in such homes without education, what will be the result to society? Boys and girls of low intelligence running the streets are most likely to become wild, uncontrolled and anti-social, forming gangs which will be a menace to society. How is their self-respect to be built up? How will they form a moral code, learn to manage their own affairs, to become self-supporting, to exercise their right to vote? Is it possible, in a modern State, to sustain life without education?

Or would they wish to segregate them in institutions, deprive them of home life, and generally deny them human rights and freedoms? If this is their idea, would it be less expensive than education? Or would it take less time and effort on the part of those who would have to look after them?

If 'training' should be suggested in place of education, this again would be no less expensive. Moreover, training, given suitable motivation, has its emotional and intellectual satisfactions, its demand for self-control and perseverance, its conscious co-ordination of the powers of mind and body in the will to achieve, and must be regarded as an aspect of education.

It seems, then, that we have to choose between letting the mentally handicapped run wild and so become a social danger, segregating them and so denying them most of the rights and freedoms of man, or educating them to take their place in

SHOULD WE ATTEMPT IT?

society as useful routine workers who, even if they will never set the Thames on fire, will at least be self-supporting and socially useful. On a purely material level then, their education would appear to be justified, if it is possible to educate them at all.

This is the point at issue. People who say it is a waste of public money to educate these children, are not considering the alternatives. They are rather giving vent to an exasperated doubt as to whether it really is possible to educate them at all.

The answer to this lies in a study of the potentialities of these mentally handicapped children, and considering these in the light of what we understand by true education. The sub-normal child, like the normal child, is a unique personality, having physiological drives, instincts and emotions which crave satisfaction, intellectual abilities, social potentialities, and the capacity to acquire modes of behaviour, interests, attitudes and skills. All of these must be developed and integrated. At each level of intelligence, however, from the normal to the defective, the vitality of these components of personality becomes weaker. This weakness is most noticeable in the intellectual skills, in the capacity for abstract thought and reasoning, in the power of controlling impulses and of adjusting to new circumstances. It is least noticeable on the level of instinct and emotional impulse, and in the capacity for manual skills, although all these also usually fall below the standard of normal achievement. In a simple environment the mentally handicapped child finds it comparatively easy to adjust, but in our complicated society he needs a great deal of help if he is to control his impulses, develop his capacities, and become a stable, contented, and socially useful adult. Without education he has a high possibility of becoming a social problem and a poorly balanced personality. If educable, then, he needs education more than those children who are more richly endowed—but is it possible to give him education? Is he educable?

If by education we mean only the acquisition of book learning, literature, science, mathematics, etc., or if we believe that only those are educated who have been able to develop considerable powers of abstract reasoning, it is quite obvious that we cannot educate these dull children, whose innate general intelligence is insufficient for the purpose. Such a conception of education, though, is too narrow. Within such a system of education, learning may indeed flourish, but it is possible that in some cases, well-adjusted and integrated personalities may fail to develop.

I would suggest that education is the process of co-ordinating the whole personality and directing all its powers towards the right ends. In this process the educator is not only the teacher, but also the parents, the cultural pattern of society—in fact, the whole environment. The active co-operation of the pupil is absolutely necessary. Passive acquiescence in being taught will never produce a truly educated person. With skill and understanding on the part of the teacher and co-operation on the part of the pupil, the co-ordination of the whole personality can very gradually be achieved. The process continues from birth to death without pause. Directing the powers of the whole personality towards the 'right ends' is differently interpreted by different schools of thought. Professor Hadfield says, 'as far as mental health is concerned, those are the right ends which give the greatest fulfilment, completeness and happiness to the personality as a whole'.

The Christian educator will claim that the greatest fulfilment, completeness and happiness is attained when the whole personality is directed Godward, in the hope of perfect union with infinite love, truth, and beauty. So the child—average or subnormal—has the right to education that he may be fitted for his high destiny. Our duty then is to help him to develop his powers to their full capacity and to show him how he may accept his limitations in obedience to the will of God. Our high privilege is to serve Christ in the person of this, the least of His little ones.

The secular humanist, on the other hand, will claim that man is the measure of all things. The right of the sub-normal child then, and our duty towards him, is such education as may help him to develop his capabilities so that he may use them in the service of humanity.

Whichever view is taken, the mentally handicapped child has an equality with the average or bright child, in that he is to develop to the fullness of his capacity. A small glass filled to the brim, or a large glass filled to the brim, both are equally full, and both the Christian and the secular humanist would recognize that a dull child pursuing the 'right ends' to his utmost capacity is a dynamic force for good.

While both the Christian and the secular humanist might claim to be pursuing the 'right ends' which will give satisfaction to the whole personality, the materialist could not validly make a like claim. He wishes to harness the human spirit in the acquisition of material goods, the greater in the service of the less. But 'the life is more than the meat', and the pursuit of material good can never give fulfilment, completeness and happiness to the higher powers of the human personality. Materialistic education is bound, sooner or later, to lead to frustration, incompleteness, and the substitution of pleasure for happiness.

On the grounds then of social expediency, Christianity, or humanitarianism it is necessary and right to attempt to educate the dull child. Is he capable of education in this wider sense? Can his personality become stable, integrated, and directed towards the right ends?

I do not doubt the possibility. Experience with a C stream in an ordinary school, and mentally handicapped children of all ages in Special Schools has convinced me that this work can be done, and that it is well worth doing. For the child's sake and for our own, though, we must recognize that in every direction his progress will be limited by his low intelligence level. We must not hope to raise this level, but must be ready to work within it, teaching him to make the best use of what abilities he has. We hope that he may learn to read and write, but we shall not regard him as a failure if this is beyond him. Education includes, but is not limited to, the 3 R's. Many a medieval craftsman produced beautiful work which still inspires us today. Could we then call him uneducated, even though it is unlikely that he could read? So with our dull and defective children. They may not be able to read, but what they can do they should be encouraged to do with all their might. If they can gradually become stable characters and conscientious workers, supporting themselves by the labour of their hands, and causing no anxiety to the community, who can deny them the means to achieve this end? Some may fail, may become unemployable, delinquents or social misfits, but these failures are known at every level of intelligence. In achieving stability, however, our dull children will need more help. They are slower in gaining control over their impulses, and they need supervision and wise control for longer than children of average intelligence. Left to themselves they will not very easily learn to adjust to their environment and to accept the standards of society. For these reasons they are in more urgent need of education than those who are more capable of helping themselves.

Joyce was admitted to a special school at about seven and a half years of age. Her mental age was five and her I.Q. 66. She was a heavily built, awkward child, with large clumsy hands, and a perpetually running nose. There was a history of mental defect in her family. During the war she was evacuated for part of the time, but when she rejoined our group she appeared very dull indeed. Up to the age of sixteen years she hardly learned to read, and was never able to do more in number than add units, although she was fairly able with shopping. In all her school life her mental age progressed only eight months, so that, when she left us at sixteen, her mental age was five years and eight months and her I.Q. was 37. If it had not been war time she would, of course, have been sent to an occupation centre.

Yet, in spite of her very low intelligence level, education was not wasted on Joyce. She learned to be punctual, tidy and clean, and because she was able to do odd jobs in a practical, sensible manner, she had a definite place in the school community. When we praised one girl for good needlework, and another for having made a beautiful doll, we never forgot to praise Joyce for her steady work at the odd jobs. So her self-respect was built up, together with her position in society. There was an episode when she began to hang about in the black-out and owned to having had sexual intercourse with various boys. We were able to deal with this by talking it over with her, and enlisting the co-operation of her mother, who was well meaning but inefficient. Her respect for us, together with her mother's support, was sufficient to pull her back upon the straight and narrow path. Without the influence of her school, what would have become of her? By the time she left us her stability was such that she was recommended for a laundry job and has held it ever since (over five years). Thus a potential menace to society was able to develop into a stable self-supporting member of the community, happy and well adjusted within the limits of her intellectual capacity.

We may then have dull but employable E.S.N. adolescents, who, with adequate supervision, will become self-supporting, self-respecting members of the community, and capable of achieving a happy, useful and purposeful life. Or we may have in their place frustrated, poorly adjusted personalities, failures and delinquents, a danger to society and to themselves unless they are segregated in institutions, where they drag along until death releases them. Both will cost money, time and effort, in the first case spent in educating them, and in the second case in supporting them in institutions or prisons.

In which case is the money, skill and effort more worthily spent?

Chapter II

THE DEVELOPMENT OF MENTALLY HANDICAPPED CHILDREN AND THE CRITERION BY WHICH THEY SHOULD BE SELECTED FOR SPECIAL SCHOOL TREATMENT

Children are recommended for statutory examination by the school medical officer, by their parents, by head teachers, by child guidance clinics, by hospitals and juvenile courts. Whatever their record of delinquency or educational backwardness they should be considered for special school treatment on the grounds of low intelligence only. Neither the criterion of backwardness without reference to its cause, nor that of social inefficiency is acceptable, and still less that of behaviour disorder. Poor intelligence (I.Q. 50–70) will necessarily be accompanied by educational backwardness, but the latter may exist without the former. Backwardness may be due to one or more of many causes. Physical conditions, for example, defects of sight or hearing, toxic conditions from septic tonsils, anaemia, fatigue from over-exertion, lack of proper sleep or nourishment may be the chief cause of trouble. It may be due to absence from school, either frequent or prolonged; to special disabilities in reading or arithmetic, to poor or unsympathetic teaching, or, more rarely, to emotional disturbances. The child whose backwardness is due to low intelligence usually shows very early signs of slow development. I knew one mentally handicapped child who, at four years old, was carried sitting on her aunt's arm, and who was able neither to speak nor to walk. Both speech and walking developed eventually, and at the age of eleven years her I.Q. was 54.

In 1949 and 1950 I investigated the ages at which the children in my school had begun to speak and walk. The findings were as follows:

		Speech		Walking	
		1949	1950	1949	1950
No. of cases investigated		37	43	41	42
Began under 12 months		—	—	2	—
,,	1–2 years	7	10	24	29
,,	2–3 ,,	13	14	11	13
,,	3–4 ,,	4	5	4	—
,,	4–5 ,,	3	1	—	—
,,	5–6 ,,	2	3	—	—
,,	6–7 ,,	5	6	—	—
,,	7+ ,,	3	4	—	—
Average Age		3–4 yrs.	3–4 yrs.	2 yrs.	1–2 yrs.

In most cases the child is not 'clean and dry' as early as a child of average intelligence. It is necessary that these developmental ages should be considered when the causes of backwardness are being investigated.

An investigation of the family history and the social background is also necessary before the child is labelled 'mentally handicapped'. This is discussed more fully in the section on 'Social background and parents' attitudes'.

The investigation of background, family conditions and developmental history is so important that, in my opinion, it is not sufficient to ask the mother a set of questions at the interview, but the home should be visited by a social worker, and her report read before the child is examined. The child's head teacher is asked to state known home conditions but this is insufficient. One of the weaknesses of our educational system is that there is too little contact between the school and the home. The parents may visit the school, but how often does the school visit the home, and find out at first hand what atmosphere and material conditions prevail there? Before any such important event as the statutory examination, this visiting should be done. Generally it is impracticable for a teacher to do it, but a social worker should certainly be asked to report.

Then the child who is educationally backward should be given a careful test of intelligence. The importance of this test, and of the manner in which it is administered, cannot be over-stressed. A diagnosis is about to be made which will affect the child's whole life, and the greatest care should be exerted. If, as a result of this test, the child's intelligence quotient is found to be between 50 and 70 (or 75) he should, in most cases, be given a trial in a special E.S.N. school.

The careful investigation of the home background should help to discover one class to which this rule should be applied with the utmost caution—but, unfortunately it is this very class which is usually hustled into the special school. I mean a small but important class of children with genuine emotional problems, which manifest themselves in behaviour disorders. These children may or may not be mentally handicapped, but either they have felt themselves to be deprived of protective love, or they have been spoiled or neglected, inconsistently treated, or they have been brought up in inharmonious homes, or by inefficient parents, and for one or another reason they have developed behaviour problems, rooted in emotional disturbance. If a child is obviously bright, he probably finds himself eventually at a child guidance clinic, or if he is violently anti-social, in a school for maladjusted children or even in an approved school.

Sometimes, however, this emotional disturbance is found in children of low average intelligence. In some of these cases it appears to have the effect of dulling or paralysing the child's ability to use the intelligence which he actually possesses. The result of this is not only backwardness, but a failure to do himself justice in the intelligence test. So, while a backward child who is well adjusted may be correctly assessed, one in a state of emotional disturbance may fail to use his powers to their full capacity, and what is measured will be not his actual intelligence, but the extent of his failure to harness the innate ability which is his.

Whether the child is anti-social and unco-operative so that he will not respond, or whether he is withdrawn and repressed and so fully occupied with his own personal problems that he cannot respond, his apparent I.Q. is likely to be within the special school range. Yet to send him to a special school is a very poor solution of his difficulties. He needs a deeper and more fundamental treatment. His social background, home difficulties and personal problems should be very carefully investigated, for it is essential to deal with these deep roots before any attempt is made to deal with his backwardness, which, together with his apparently low I.Q., is a symptom only and not a cause. Later his specific difficulties in arithmetic and reading should be diagnosed and remedial treatment given.

Such children, when given special school treatment, may blossom out in the free atmosphere, and, helped by the individual attention to compensate for their feeling of being unwanted, they may show their true level quite quickly. For example, one of my pupils whose test in August 1949 indicated a mental age of 7 years 3 months and an I.Q. of 74, by July 1950 had arrived at a mental age of 9 years 2 months and an I.Q. of 83.

Others may appear to have a low intelligence level for a very long time, and may gradually climb upwards, or may suddenly 'find themselves' after years of misunderstanding. The following quotations from my records illustrate cases of this type:

AGNES

Date of Test	Mental age	I.Q.
3.7.47.	5 yrs. 10 mths.	72
22.6.48.	6 ,, 4 ,,	70
29.3.49.	7 ,, 4 ,,	75
30.11.49.	8 ,, — ,,	76
10.7.50.	9 ,, 2 ,,	83

JIMMIE

Date of Test	Mental age	I.Q.
28.1.47.	5 yrs. 8 mths.	73
22.1.48	6 ,, 4 ,,	72
11.11.48.	6 ,, 10 ,,	70
25.4.49.	7 ,, 2 ,,	71
21.12.49	9 ,, 6 ,,	88

RONALD

Date of Test	Mental age	I.Q.
15.5.46.	3 yrs. 8 mths.	45
13.3.47	4 ,, – ,,	45
4.3.48.	5 ,, 6 ,,	55
25.11.48.	5 ,, 10 ,,	54
15.7.49.	7 ,, 8 ,,	67
14.6.50.	11 ,, – ,,	89

These children, and we have others who are in the same category, are out of place in a special school, and we sense this even while their I.Q. still appears to be very low. We do what we can for them until they are deascertained,[1] but even though we run a 'maladjusted' group we are not happy about them. We may help them to discover and overcome some of their difficulties but although this must be the first step in their treatment, we feel that it should not have to take place in a special E.S.N. school. If their problem had been correctly diagnosed in the first place, they should never have been sent to us, although special provision needs to be made for them, e.g. as maladjusted.

It often happens, though, that children who have been deascertained show a great discrepancy between mental age and attainment. They have learned to use their intelligence, but to make up their loss in attainment they need remedial teaching in a very small group. If we could pass them on to such classes, their readiness to profit by them might be some justification for their period in a special school. Instead of this, we have to throw them out into a system which has no place for

[1] This very ungainly word is generally used for the process of deeming a special school child fit to return to ordinary school.

them. They will probably go into large classes, where educational attainment is necessary if they are to hold their heads above water. They do not belong to the special E.S.N. school, but they can find no place among the milling crowds into which they will now be cast. What is to become of them? One point emerges very clearly; they should have been dealt with as emotionally disturbed children from the beginning, and should never have entered the special E.S.N. school at all. For this reason I believe that, while backward children (I.Q. 50–70) should normally be considered for special school treatment, it is of importance that those who also show behaviour disorders, whether of a violently anti-social kind, or of a withdrawn, repressed, emotionless kind, should be reconsidered very carefully, and, if necessary, given treatment other than that offered by the special school.

Chapter III

SOCIAL BACKGROUND
AND PARENTS' ATTITUDES

A special school serves a very much wider area than an ordinary school, and the home conditions are very varied. Many of the fathers are unskilled labourers, but others may be journalists, managers of departments, buyers in large stores, master tailors, and one whose boy is in my school is the owner of a large guest-house. The homes of my pupils range from a luxury flat to a flat with three tiny rooms in a tumbledown slum. Some parents speak with B.B.C. accents, and others find it impossible to say a few words without bad language or blasphemy. Some mothers are like fashion plates, others are gallantly trying to make ends meet, and keep the home together, in spite of careless, lazy, or indifferent husbands who spend in the public-house or on the dogs what the family needs. Other mothers are careless, untidy and dirty, and have no care for home or children. Others are well meaning, but quite incapable.

The size of the family is, in my school at least, no larger than that from which my normal club children come. In 1950 I investigated the family conditions of the fifty children who were then in my school and my findings are given below:

Size of Family			Position of E.S.N. Child			
1 child	3 families		First in family	14	E.S.N. children	
2 children	13 ,,		Second ,, ,,	14	,,	,,
3 ,,	19 ,,		Third ,, ,,	10	,,	,,
4 ,,	4 ,,		Fourth ,, ,,	2	,,	,,
5 ,,	2 ,,		Fifth ,, ,,	3	,,	,,
6 ,,	3 ,,		Sixth ,, ,,	2	,,	,,
7 ,,	1 ,,		Seventh,, ,,	—	,,	,,
8 ,,	2 ,,		Eighth ,, ,,	1	,,	,,
9 ,,	2 ,,		Ninth ,, ,,	2	,,	,,
10 ,,	1 ,,		Tenth ,, ,,	1	,,	,,

Average size of family of E.S.N. children = 2.5
,, ,, ,, ,, ,, normal club children = 3

The apparent intelligence of the parents is widely varied, as is their will to co-operate with the school and their ability to do so. Most are friendly and anxious to do their best; some are pleasant enough when we meet, but are, on the whole, indifferent; very few are hostile. When I first came into the work, it used to be said that the parents were very largely hostile and unco-operative. Conditions have changed, there is no longer a stigma attached to the special school, and the parents are usually very pleasant indeed. Some are rather unstable, and they easily 'blow up' but I have always found that, even though they may come in like lions, they almost invariably go out like lambs. Their intentions are to be friendly, but we must understand their difficulties and their temperament, and we must respect their position as parents. We teachers are, after all, the servants of the parents as really as is a tutor in a noble family. It is for us to respect them before we expect them to respect us.

I have always been accustomed to visiting some of the homes, and now I am gradually and systematically visiting all of them. So far I have always been received with a very gracious welcome. Occasionally our conversation has taken place on the doorstep, but I know that it is not always convenient in these very small and crowded homes, to take an unexpected guest into the living-room. The husband, perhaps, is eating his meal, or the place has not been tidied up, or maybe it is a poverty-stricken place, and the mother shrinks from letting a visitor see the few poor sticks of furniture which make her home. But almost always the parents are glad of an informal chat on their own ground. Their attitude to us as teachers is usually above reproach, but what of their attitude to the mentally handicapped child? I have found that this varies considerably, and that it often is connected with the intelligence or lack of intelligence of the siblings. In my school out of thirty-eight cases investigated, three children had siblings who had won scholarships, twenty-five had siblings of average intelligence, i.e. they were able to keep up in ordinary primary or secondary schools, and ten had some siblings who were mentally handicapped and some whose intelligence was average or good.

Some parents who have one mentally handicapped child in an average or intelligent family, tend to look on him as the 'cuckoo in the nest'. Their pride is hurt. How could *they* have managed to produce such a child? They are afraid, too, that there may be some sub-normality in themselves which the child has inherited. This is so unthinkable that they hide the fear from themselves by blaming the child. He *could* be different if he *would*, they say, and they expect more of the child than he can ever hope to accomplish. They compare his achievements with those of the other children, they point out to him that his younger brothers and sisters are leaving him behind, and generally make him feel that they do not accept him, and that he has no place in their affections.

Tom is in such a position. His eldest sister won a scholarship, and is hoping to become a teacher. The other children are all doing well at school. The parents are intelligent, although the father is shiftless and boastful. He is in and out of jobs continually, and spends his money, when he has any, on the dogs. The mother is hard worked with such a husband and a family of ten to wash, mend, and cook for. In addition to all this she goes out cleaning, to make ends meet. She is too worn out to have 'time for' a backward child. His slow ways and his nervous giggle (which we never hear at school) get 'on her nerves', and both she and her husband nag the child because of his inability to come up to their standards. Our problem in this family, and in many like cases, is to get the parents to accept the child as he is. How far they are capable of changing their attitude I do not know. In their present circumstances it will be very difficult. The mother is worn out, and the father is really ill in addition to being selfish and indifferent, so that they are not likely to be able to use sympathy and imagination in dealing with Tom. Even with the best will in the world, who would feel able to cope with Tom's difficulties, while babies were crying, and the toddlers were under everybody's feet, and the week's washing was waiting to be done, and the shopping and cooking had not been started. . . . Personally I would not like to try it.

While the fairly intelligent parent may tend to blame the child rather than to accept his disability (not realizing that this is a defence mechanism), the very dull parent will often fail to recognize that the child is sub-normal at all. This type of parent is the most likely to object to her child's transfer to a special school. It is unnecessary. The child is very intelligent, but suffers from 'nerves'. Mrs. Jones was such a parent. She was obviously of very limited intelligence, and was temperamental and unstable. Her elder boy was at a special school, and they had ruined him! He was bright before he began to copy the silly boys there. Now her younger boy, Tim, had been assigned to a special E.S.N. school and her indignation knew no bounds. She would go to prison before he should come. However he came, and Mrs. Jones settled down quite happily. Tim, however, proved ineducable. At ten years of age he could hardly make himself understood, and his I.Q. was only 40. He had the habit of clutching the little girls round the throat and kissing them. The more they struggled the tighter he gripped, so that it was necessary to have him excluded. Mrs. Jones was as indignant as before. He would not hurt the girls, he only wanted to kiss them because he was kind. Just as poor Tom cannot come up to the standards set by his family, so Tim cannot fall short of them, whatever he does.

The better-off mother usually fusses and 'babies' the mentally handicapped child, until he becomes even more dependent than he need be. Some mothers love to have a permanent baby, and they grieve to see even their normal children grow up. Such a mother finds satisfaction in the prolonged babyhood of a sub-normal child, and she stifles whatever ability he may actually possess. Other mothers fail to understand the child's potentialities, and handicap him by a well-meant, but mistaken, desire to compensate him for his disabilities. So the child is indulged and spoilt, and kept a baby, and while this continues he will never be able to take his place in school or at work.

Jean was such a child. Her mother fully realized her handicap, but could not be persuaded that she must be taught to do things for herself, and to give way to other children on occasion. So Jean would expect to be waited on by the other girls, although she was eleven years old. She would shrug and sulk if she did not get her own way, and if she saw trouble coming on account of her own spiteful behaviour, she would immediately say 'I am not well.' Another girl of thirteen years old, I.Q. 67, had been brought up to feel that she was not bound by ordinary rules, and could have whatever privileges she wanted. She would refuse the school dinner saying that she could have better food at home. It was pointed out that all the other children, as well as all the teachers, ate the dinner, although presumably they also could get better food at home. She replied, 'Yes, madam, but *I'm* different'.

This sense of being different and far superior to other people, comes from the parents' feeling of the child's inferiority, and the spoiling which, they hope, will compensate the child. This is very evident in the attitude of Sally and her mother. Sally's father was a negro, who, I believe, has deserted his family. Her mother is a white woman, who now lives with her own mother and brothers. From her attitude it is apparent that she feels a deep sense of inferiority on Sally's behalf, not on account of her mental handicap, which she steadfastly refuses to acknowledge, but on account of her colour. Nothing will convince her that the child is not being victimized because she is not white. In reaction to this quite groundless feeling of her inferiority, she insists that Sally is superior to all the other children, that the school is not good enough for her, and that she has no desire for her to do well in the school, since she should not be with us at all. This idea she has purposely and consciously communicated to the child, so that she has no incentive to get on and do

SOCIAL BACKGROUND AND PARENTS' ATTITUDES 23

well. She despises the school, the teachers, and the other children. This tends to produce the very result the mother fears. The other children were glad to have Sally, and to make much of her when she first came, but she was so unready to make friends with them, and so openly despised them, that she is easily the most unpopular child in the school, not because of her colour, but because of the attitude her mother instilled into her. We have done our best to explain all this to Sally's mother, and after a long talk she became friendly and co-operative, but she has not found it possible to undo the harm she has done to the child's attitude. Her change of front simply means to Sally that her mother has gone over to the enemy, leaving her to battle alone. It is probable, too, that though the mother's attitude to the school has changed, she has been unable to change her deep feeling of shame at Sally's colour. It is likely that there was such an upset at the time of Sally's birth, that she will never be able to take a normal view of the matter. There is little doubt, though, that she has done almost irreparable harm to the girl by over compensating for her feeling of inferiority on her behalf.

Even more difficult from the child's point of view is a lack of co-operation between its parents. Sometimes this is shown in differences in discipline, sometimes in the rejection of the child by one parent while the other accepts him. Alan was born two years after his sister, while his father was in the army. He was backward in walking and speaking, but not very noticeably. When he was two years old, a flying bomb fell on the house next door, and Alan, his mother and his sister were buried in the ruins of their own house. After this experience both Alan and his sister seemed rather backward, and Alan was always ailing. His mother naturally made more fuss of him, and he became very spoilt, and extremely difficult. Then his father came home, only to find that his son, on whom he had built great hopes, was both backward and dreadfully spoilt. His ordinary school had not a good word to say for him and his father was disappointed and disgusted. He was a successful man himself, and was inordinately proud of his success. He wanted a son worthy of his own idea of himself. Seeing that the boy had been 'ruined' by indulgence, he rushed to the other extreme and the child was bewildered. Alan feels now that, while his mother and grandparents are 'for him' his father is against him. Alan has an I.Q. of 72 but is very unstable. He not only feels the insecurity due to his parents' disagreement over discipline, but he also has to cope with his natural feeling of having been pushed out of his place by his younger brother, after having been himself the baby and the only son for six years.

Alan's father genuinely wants to do his best for his son, but, having a preconceived notion of what his son should be like, he refuses to accept him as he is. The effect on Alan is the feeling of rejection.

Some among the parents of our mentally handicapped children are domineering bullies. Robert's father was said to be 'neurasthenic'. He certainly could not work, and the neat, anxious little wife earned what little she could, and in spite of their very real poverty, she managed to keep Robert beautifully neat and tidy. His clothes were very old, but where most of our children would have had holes, he had wonderfully neat and beautiful darns. Robert was terrified of his father, who was very stern and harsh. Perhaps it was his own feeling of failure which made him terrorize the child. It is so easy to be 'big' when one has only a helpless child to deal with, and so strengthening to the esteem of one of life's 'failures'. It may be that the man was only treating his boy as he himself had been treated, and that he thought it the right way to bring up children. There was nothing we could do, except talk to the father, but as far as I know that was quite useless. The effect upon Robert was to make him into as big a bully as his father. He would make a slave of a weaker boy, was extremely spiteful, and really was rather a menace to the other children. Yet he was quite

SOCIAL BACKGROUND AND PARENTS' ATTITUDES 25

servile before anybody stronger than himself. His attitude was a direct reflection of that of his father, and he was not likely, with his very poor mentality, I.Q. 55, to be able to change it. If his father could have changed, a great deal of good would have been done to the boy, but as his father was neurasthenic, it is very unlikely that he would have the will or the energy to alter his ways.

Among our very strangest cases of parental attitudes is that of Diana. She came to us at the age of six years, I.Q. 64. She had been in a residential hospital for mental defectives from babyhood, but her parents had to have her home, against their will, at the age of six. She was a tiny thing when she first came home, bright and cheerful, beautifully dressed in the clothes she had brought from the home, friendly and even too fond of notice. All went well for a time, then her father came to ask if she had been 'saying things' about her parents' treatment. He seemed very anxious for her welfare, and we assured him that nobody would take notice of the tales of so young and so backward a child. Then her mother came up and immediately we became suspicious. The mother was a cripple; she was very tidy, spoke well and seemed intelligent, but there was a withdrawn, closed-in expression on her face which rather made us doubt her. She complained that Diana was very dirty, and soiled her clothes and her bed. Diana was never dirty at school, but was able to attend to herself quite well.

Again and again the parents came up, always with complaints which we did not really believe. We noticed, though, that the child was looking very pale and anxious, and had lost her bouncing, cheerful manner. She began to steal other children's lunch, and would say, as we had been warned that she would, that she had had no breakfast. She began to cry when the guide took her home, and asked to stay with the guide and not go home 'to that mummy'. She would cry when she passed a baker's shop on the way to school. The guide bought her a roll, and reported that Diana devoured it ravenously. We asked a visitor to investigate, and it was simply reported that the home was spotless! Her father came to see me and complained again of the child's behaviour. In addition to the former complaints there was a new one. It seemed that her mother had found Diana standing in front of a long mirror, making long scratches on her bare body with a pin. Although I know that such things may happen in certain cases of neurosis or mental trouble, I would have looked for it in the case of a withdrawn person (like Diana's mother) rather than in the case of a cheerful active little person like Diana herself. Certainly she had lost a great deal of her cheerfulness, but still she did not seem the type to indulge in such practices. I asked her how she got the scratches and she said her mother had done it. Again I asked the visitor to investigate, and again all the sympathy was with the mother. Then we found that Diana had circular bruises on her back and seat, which, she said, had been caused by the wire mattress on which she was sleeping. She said she had no thick mattress, but slept on the springs. Again I asked for an investigation, and again there was no sympathy with the child. The visitor had seen the mattress which she had ruined, lying in the garden. It was completely unfit for use. So she was lying on folded rugs on the wire spring, and he did not see what else the poor mother could do. The home, except for the damage wrought by this child, was spotless! A spotless home covers a multitude of sins in the official view!

Meanwhile the parents were continuing to complain, and begged that the child might be sent away. Although we at the school had nothing but our 'hunch' to go on, we were convinced that a case had been very carefully built up by the parents in the hope of getting rid of the child. Personally, I was afraid to leave the little thing there any longer, because I felt that the mother was not quite normal, in her attitude to this one child. Her other children, much older, were welcome in the home, but this child was not. The father, I thought, was the mother's dupe, and he only knew what she told him . . . until, one day, when the child was in the bus with the guide, she begged the guide not to take her home to 'that mummy'. Suddenly the father, who had also been in the bus, came up and thrust his face right up to the child's, and said, 'Now I've caught you at it at last.' The child screamed with fright, and the guide came straight back to me and said that something must be done. Again I begged for the child to be removed from that home. I knew that was what the parents had been trying to accomplish, but for the child's sake they must have their wish. At last the thing was done, and Diana went to an orphanage near the school. Immediately she began to pick up. She no longer asked for food, she became lively and bouncing as she used to be, and she no longer cried to stay with the guide, but was very happy to go back to the 'home' at the end of the day. The 'home' was really for normal children, but Diana fitted in very well among them. When I rang up the Matron she said that Diana seemed to her a normal child (probably because she looked much younger than her six years), and that she had neither wetted nor dirtied the bed since she had been there. She has gone now to a residential school, but unless we had followed our 'hunch', she would still have been living in that spotless home, in those unspeakable conditions. A mentally handicapped child is so very helpless in such circumstances, and although I do not think there are many cases of that abnormal attitude on the part of the parents, yet it does sometimes happen, and we are the only ones who can afford some measure of protection to such children.

Sometimes we find that parents are well meaning, but careless and incapable. These are the less intelligent parents. Brian and Michael come from such a home. Their father is dead, their stepfather takes little interest in them, and their mother is a fat, untidy, rather stupid and dilatory person, who loves them noisily at times, and screams at them at others. She has a good many children, and is good-naturedly careless of them all. She says she does not want any more children because 'those you get nowadays aren't worth having'. She is thoroughly careless, slovenly and incapable, but there is a certain rough show of mother love, and though the children are already showing delinquent tendencies without, apparently, causing her the slightest worry, yet she is immediately up in arms if anybody upsets them, and they have a certain sense of security in her protection.

Some careless parents do not even give this feeling of security to their children, but are bound up in their own affairs, drinking, quarrelling, changing partners and settling down again, spending on the dogs, and generally living such a full life (of a sort), that they have scarcely time to trouble how their children fill their lives. Mrs. Smith is such a parent. She was always slovenly and her home was always full of children crawling in deep dirt. Everything was on the floor, crusts, lumps of salt, forks, broken toys, rags and dirty clothes, and the children played among it all, eating a crust if they fancied it, throwing it back among the rubbish when they had had enough. Her husband was quite different, but eventually he committed suicide. Mrs. Smith soon 'settled down' again. She had at least six children, and 'Yorkie' settled in with her, bringing two children of his own to swell the crowd. They live in the tiniest flat in a slum. How they all get in is a mystery.

'Yorkie', as he calls himself, is a delightful man to talk to. He bought a white goat from a sailor, and put it out to pasture on the little bit of grass in the local 'buildings'. He said he had bought it so that Bill, who was at my school, could have plenty of milk to drink. This was typical of 'Yorkie'. He was talking to me, so the goat had to be for the child in my school! He was full of tales of large sums of money which were waiting for him to collect, but, apparently, he was spurning them all. He could not marry Mrs. Smith, he told me, because he was already married 'to a real lady'. If she came down the street at that moment, he was not fit to touch her shoe. He would not marry Mrs. Smith if he could, for 'if she's like she is now, what would she be like if we were married?' Mrs. Smith and Yorkie had two or three mutual children, so he did not want to leave her. Some of Mrs. Smith's older boys had been in trouble with the police, and Yorkie would have liked them sent to a 'home' so that 'they would know what it is to be without a stepfather'. In spite of the irregularity of his position, I believe that the man had done some good for those older boys, in the early days, at any rate. I used to see him going to work every morning, and Tom (the third boy) used to accompany him as far as he could, looking up at him with real hero worship, while the man looked down with interest and affection. I did not then know Yorkie, although I knew Tom, but I used to find their absorbtion in one another most attractive.

What happened to spoil it? Drink, I think, and Mrs. Smith's jealous tantrums. I have seen Yorkie walking down the long road, carrying a dead rabbit, while Mrs. Smith followed at a respectful distance, screaming abuse. When the man stopped and looked round, she would stop. When he went on, she would follow, still shouting at him. At last they reached the main road, and soon after I saw them on the top of a bus, as happy as larks together, and greeting me as an old friend. Yorkie told me that his trouble is drink, but that he never uses bad language in front of a woman, and has had many a fight with men in a pub, because they have used obscenity in front of Mrs. Smith.

From such homes as this, with their irregular morals, their odd confusion of standards, their mixture of three families (at least) within the framework of one family, their drunkenness, boasting, lying, and dishonesty, their quarrelling and disharmony, come some of our children. Can we wonder that they have no sense of security, that they lie, truant and steal, that they cannot assimilate our standards of friendly co-operation, social living and truthfulness? The parents' attitudes are almost inevitably reflected in those of their children, and the child from a careless, amoral or vicious home is bound to carry the scars at least. With our highly suggestible children, it is likely that those who come from such families will not be able to withstand their home influence, and will themselves found new 'problem families'.

So far the parents' attitudes discussed, have all been in some measure detrimental to the best interests of the children. I would not wish to imply that this is always, or even usually, the case. The few cases where parents' attitudes or home conditions are unsatisfactory are in the minority, but they tend to stand out more prominently because of their abnormality. Many of our children have good, intelligent and loving parents, who are anxious to co-operate with the school, and to help the child, as far as they can, to make the very best use of what potentialities he has. They provide a stable background, plenty of interesting occupations in the home, supervision, a wise control, and, most important of all, the security of a protective love, without an unwise indulgence.

If this were not so, the fate of these children when they leave school at the age of sixteen, and have to take their place in competition with average and intelligent adolescents, would not bear contemplation. Unless most of the parents were doing their job fairly efficiently, it would be essential to provide protected employment and hostel accommodation for most of our mentally handicapped adolescents. As it is, I think it should be provided for those who are very unstable themselves, and for those who have a very unsatisfactory home background. Both of these drift from one job to another, and are in great need of a strong stable adult who can help and advise them continuously. Their demands are more than a club leader or visiting social worker can answer. They need a continual support and control. This I think, should be the next step in the care of the mentally handicapped. I would emphasize, however, that where the home is good (not merely spotless, but good in a wider sense) these boys and girls are far better off at home than in the more artificial and less homely atmosphere of a hostel, however good. Nothing can replace the home, but, because its influence is so very strong, the child from a really bad home is most likely to be anti-social and self-seeking. These children, although numerically few, are in most urgent need of help, and no time should be lost in making provision for them.

Many difficulties arise in the formation of parent-teacher associations, especially as the children come from such a wide area. Yet most of the parents I visited were most interested in the idea. I found that there was no day or time which would be generally acceptable, and yet I did not wish to drop the scheme. The staff and I discussed the matter very fully and decided that the most workable plan would be to invite a few parents only together, and to have a small group every two or three weeks. We pick out parents whose children provide a common problem, e.g. the problem of speech defect, of subnormality caused by epileptic tendency, of practical ability together with compete lack of interest in reading or number, or of I.Q.'s above or below special school standards. We also pick out parents who present a difficult problem to their child, the parent who treats the subnormal like a young baby, the parent who has no patience for a slow child, the over-harsh and the over-indulgent parent, and we group these together so that we can speak of discipline to the indulgent group and of gentle encouragement to the harsh group.

We invite four or five at a time, generally in the afternoon. Those who are not free during the day are invited after school hours, but we really prefer them to come while they can see the ordinary work of the school. First they are taken to visit the class teacher and to see for themselves how their child fits into his school environment. We try to pick only one or two parents for any one class, so that the teacher has time really to answer their questions. They can, if they wish, spend half an hour or more with the class teacher. Then they come as a group to have a cup of tea in the head teacher's room. Here they can discuss their problems with her, if they have not already done so individually, but, more important, they can discuss them with one another, and can share experience. If they can get to know one another, and to recognize one another's problems, they will no longer feel isolated in their difficulties, and we hope that they will lose the feeling of shame which some now feel at having a child who is sub-normal in intelligence. Although we are very glad to see the parents at any time, and always invite them for open days, etc., we feel that our most useful contact with them is in these small parent-teacher association groups. We are hoping, at least once a year, to have a full parent-teacher association meeting or social, and also to form groups of those who are interested in talks on backwardness and sub-normality. This, however, is for the future, when we have cleared the ground a little. For the moment we are concentrating on helping individual parents, meeting in small groups, to understand their own child's needs a little better, to sympathize with the like problems of other children and their parents, and to co-operate more fully in the work of the school.

Chapter IV

DELINQUENCY AMONG E.S.N. CHILDREN

Because there appears to be a good deal of delinquency among mentally handicapped children, some people have leapt to the conclusion that low intelligence is in itself a predisposing factor in delinquency. Personally I disagree with this view. Mentally handicapped children are highly suggestible, and if environmental circumstances are favourable to delinquency they are likely to become delinquent. On the other hand, while the normal child from a highly moral family, who is given care and supervision and every material necessity, may react against all this and seek adventure in delinquency, the mentally handicapped child in a similar environment is more likely to appear stable and law abiding. Because the mentally handicapped child has less inherent ability to determine his own course, I believe that environmental conditions are even more important to him than to the normal child. This, I think, is the reason for the startling improvement which children sometimes show when they enter the prepared environment of a special school. As we have seen, even their I.Q. sometimes appears to improve. For this reason also the 'social climate' of a special school is of paramount importance.

Unfortunately the environment of a dull or mentally handicapped child is very often unsatisfactory. The home, often, is poor, the parents often fail to understand the child, there is sometimes dirt, drunkenness and quarrelling, and often the children are allowed to roam the streets, making social contacts where they will. Sometimes they are the dupes of the dull and backward truanters or even the intelligent delinquents from ordinary schools, who use these highly suggestible children as catspaws. I know of one who was regularly sent into

Woolworth's to steal, while his friends waited outside to receive the goods. If anybody had been caught, it would have been the poor dupe, who hardly knew what he was doing, and certainly had no anti-social intentions. In fact, as far as he was concerned, he was doing a social act, looking only as far as his own small group, and not perceiving his obligations to a larger society.

For this reason, it is most important that children with I.Q.'s above 70 who have behaviour disorders or tendencies to delinquency should not be sent to special schools. I need hardly say that this is the very type to find its way to us! Such children often are dull and backward, but very often they have a higher degree of innate intelligence than appears in their test result, and they may work havoc among the children of lower-grade intelligence whom they will meet in a special E.S.N. school. Bill (aged ten) was such a boy. He was sent to us while awaiting a place in a residential special school. He had 'been to court' and his medical examination won him a place in a special school instead of in an approved school. He was a likeable rogue, but I doubt whether his intelligence was as low as it appeared! He came from a careless home, and had spent nights out when it pleased him. Nobody cared. He did as he liked. He usually arrived at school with a collection of goods which he had 'picked up in the kerb'. A surgeon's scalpel, a baby's rattle and a cut-glass vase was one morning's haul! When the children lined up for second helpings at dinner-time, he would work himself in at the front of the queue, when he should have been at the back, and once when he was served first, having 'jumped the queue', he remarked, 'The last shall be first.' He led the other boys into mischief. They truanted with him, and stole with him. The climax was when he took three or four boys off for a day's truancy, and they had no money. He called at a general shop, and helped himself to a siphon of soda water. None of them liked the flavour so they 'wasted it in the road'. He then took the empty siphon back to the same shop and received two shillings on it. The gang then went off, treated themselves at a coffee shop, and spent the remainder on a bus fare to Barnes. There they broke into a garage, and took a few tools. They were 'picked up' by the police, and all appeared at the juvenile court soon after. At this point I asked that Bill might be removed immediately to his residential school, as he was leading the others astray. In my opinion a great deal of the delinquency of mentally handicapped children has no more malice in it than the adventures of Bill's gang. The leader, only, is responsible (as far as he is capable of responsibility) and the others are simply incapable of withstanding his suggestions.

The normally intelligent person is also assailed by environmental influences. His moral sentiments lead him to reject these if they are not in accordance with his ideals. From within himself he is assailed by his own emotional impulses and by the repressions and complexes which have been rejected by his conscious self. His ability to deal with these impulses depends upon the strength of the organized self in the pursuit of its ideal—in fact, upon the will. He has the duty of building up his character by the exercise of his will. He may give way to his impulses and indulge in anti-social conduct, but at least he has full knowledge of, and responsibility for, what he does. He is able, to a great extent, to foresee the consequences of his acts, both in the wrong he will do to other people, in the violence he will do to his own 'self', and in the punishment he will incur. Even the person whose sentiments and ideals are socially unacceptable, is able to foresee the punishment he will bring upon himself.

The mentally handicapped child is, as I have said, less able to reject environmental influences. He is more at the mercy of his impulses, because his low intelligence makes the integration of his personality a slower and more difficult achievement. Sentiments are built up more slowly, his judgment of what is good is less sure, and he finds it more difficult to keep his ideal in mind, since he has so little power of abstract thought, and the concrete is so much more vivid to him than ideals. It is, therefore, less likely that his sentiments will be organized in conscious and continued pursuit of his ideal, his will must be correspondingly weak, and he is largely at the mercy of every momentary impulse and emotion. In addition to this he is less able than the normal child to foresee the consequences of his actions, even in such a matter as punishment to himself. He does not look forward, as a rule, but acts on the impulse of the moment. He has little conception of the wrong he may do to others, and his notion of society is usually limited to his immediate companions. We have to work to help him build up sentiments and ideals, and we have to give him a knowledge of right and wrong, but we must also understand that this knowledge may fail him when his emotional impulses call upon him to act. Within certain limits he can become a stable, integrated character, so long as he is not subjected to harmful influences, and so long as he can always rely upon a person stronger than himself. The high degree of suggestibility which is characteristic of the mentally handicapped child can work towards good conduct as well as towards bad, but there is little doubt that he will react according to the influence of the moment, and that good influence, usually in the form of supervision, control, good companions and healthy occupation must always be present if it is to be effective.

Within school these children can distinguish right from wrong, they can make judgments and act upon them, they can form ideals and pursue them, because the right influences are around them, and they are being upheld and encouraged in their choice of the right. Even so we get breakdowns in control, and regression to infantile emotional behaviour. These we are usually able to treat by giving legitimate outlets for emotional impulses, for example, free play or painting, etc. Conduct in school is usually satisfactory. The main problem of delinquency among mentally handicapped children is an out-of-school problem. Though we try to do so, it is in many cases almost impossible to give them a defence against the situations they will meet after school. Some of them are almost bound to succumb either to environmental influences, or to the promptings of their own emotional impulses. Parents may be co-operative and many provide suitable occupations in a comfortable home—and their children are safe. Other parents are at work. They may appear interested in their child, but if he goes home to an empty flat, with nobody to welcome and nobody to control him, what is their interest worth?

Terence was such a boy. He had a good, though somewhat over-strict, mother, who went out to work. Terence left an empty house in the morning, and returned to an empty house after school. He was a very lively youngster who looked exactly like 'Just William'. He was a sore trial to all his teachers, but yet he was thoroughly likeable. He had considerable verbal and dramatic ability and could keep his whole class enthralled while he made up stories, acting them as he went along. This same ability led him to make up wonderful excuses when he was caught in some crime, and when one imaginative excuse was exposed as a fraud, he would embark upon another without a blush. At school we could give him plenty of outlets for his talents but his home did not. When he came from home in the morning he would often bring some of his parents' property with him. Once he brought a great watch which had belonged to his grandfather, and it was seen no more. He said he had hidden it in a hole in the wall near the cinema—but this was probably one of his yarns. Instead of going home to an empty house, he often used to prefer a walk round the market 'knocking off' fruit, etc., from the stalls. Sometimes, with another of our boys whose mother was also at work, he would walk round Woolworth's, picking up oddments as he went. He knew perfectly well that stealing is wrong, and he certainly knew what to expect if his mother found out—yet moral standards were abstract and could not enter into competition with the impulse to take what he saw in front of him, and possible retribution was too far away to exert any influence over him. I saw him once about to enter the store. For some reason he was accustomed to saying to an adult, 'Please, is this Woolworth's?' He had probably once been treated to an ice on the strength of such an encounter. However, without looking up he walked straight up to me and said, 'Please, is this Woolworth's?' He looked up, and the frozen horror on his face proved that he knew he was there for no acceptable purpose! Yet where was the child to go? Who would go home to an empty house while the shops are bright and warm and full of people? Once in the shop, the rest follows. His mother came to see me about his habits, and I told her that the only hope was for her to give up her afternoon job, meet him, and take him home and provide interests there for him. She did this, and he has perforce given up his delinquency. If she had been less co-operative, he would almost certainly have found himself in a juvenile court.

Other boys have parents who neither know nor care what they do, as long as they themselves are not bothered by them. A group of these boys entered an empty house, or a warehouse, and had a fine game there. In the course of the game they found and opened a gas-meter. All scrambled and struggled together to get the money. Then they went out to spend it. Two took the next day off from school to celebrate their good fortune, and spent the day in feasting and an orgy of buying small toys, etc. The third came to school with a new bow and arrow, and a pocket full of shillings and pennies, which were promptly confiscated. The extent of their moral responsibility can be seen from his attitude. I explained that the money was stolen and he could not have it, and, with difficulty he agreed to part with it. He could see no reason, however, for losing the bow and arrow which had been bought with some of the money. Even after I had explained the position, he still came to ask for it before going home.

The boys were later interviewed by a police officer in the

DELINQUENCY

presence of their fathers. They described where they had been and what they had done, and were ready to take the officer to the scene of the crime. When asked, 'Did you know it was wrong to take the money?' they said they did, and in theory they did know—but not in practice. Certainly they would have decamped if they had seen a policeman coming, but I think that while even at the time they realized it was not safe, they had no realization that it was morally wrong. They were in the grip of their impulses, and each was reacting upon the other. Retribution might come, but that was a far-away thought, unless it had happened to materialize in the form of a policeman. What those boys need is a good home, with a mother who will be waiting for them when they return, and parents who will share their interests and help them to use their evenings pleasurably but innocently. Unfortunately none of those three boys has such a home and parents.

Jimmie has a home where his parents are always quarrelling. His father and elder brother are violent to his mother. His middle brother is often spiteful to him. His married sister periodically 'packs up her husband' (to use Jimmie's expression) and comes to live at home. She is uncouth and rough and the home influence seems worse than ever when she is there. Jimmie is terrified that his mother will leave home, as she threatens to do when her eldest son 'goes for' her—his one worry is that she will go and leave him behind. During his short life (now aged eleven) Jimmie has been involved in many anti-social acts. Once, at seven years, he with two other boys took a baby to a piece of waste land and threw stones at it. Soon after, he truanted from school, and stole two bicycles from other children on the way home. Later he stole another bicycle—and later still, another. He has been on probation, and has spent a fortnight in a remand home. At one time his behaviour was so violent that we feared for the safety of the other children. All through we have tried to get the co-operation of his mother, but she has simply ignored our invitations to come and discuss what can be done. If he plays truant, she will write a note to say she kept him at home. On all occasions she shields him from the consequences of his actions, while refusing to exert a preventive control. What can be done? It would perhaps seem a case for a residential school and yet there is such a bond of love between the mother and the child, unwisely though she may express it, that more harm than good would probably be done by removing him from the security of her affection. What, then, is the answer to the problem?

Often it is answered by probation. Yet probation depends so entirely upon the co-operation of the child, that it is difficult to see how it can be fully efficacious in the case of a mentally handicapped child, who is incapable of giving the intelligent co-operation which is essential to its success. I think the only answer to the problem is preventive supervision after school hours. Where this is given in the home the ideal is achieved. Where this is not given in the home, special clubs or play centres for mentally handicapped children are needed. These children are less able than normal children to employ their leisure profitably, and yet they are given much more leisure in which to get into mischief. From three-thirty p.m. till bedtime they have to amuse themselves, and they have so few resources. The boy with nothing to do, and no resources, obviously will wander off, and get into mischief by doing damage to property, entering premises and stealing, etc. The girl with nothing to occupy her (rather a rare phenomenon, since a girl is so useful in the home) may steal, but, as she gets older, is more likely to seek sex adventures. As these children grow they have the same instinctive sex impulses which a normal adolescent finds it so difficult to control. The sub-normal child, however, has to attempt to control these emotional impulses with a mentality which is comparable to that of a normal six- or eight-year-old child. Clubs and play centres, open from three-thirty to seven-thirty p.m., where interests, hobbies, games and entertainments

DELINQUENCY

would be provided, should help to keep our boys from wandering into trouble, and our older girls from seeking adventure on street corners and in dark alleys. In the case of junior children such centres might prevent that first drifting towards socially unacceptable behaviour.

Among the children in my own junior school the actual number of known delinquents is comparatively small. From September 1947 when the school opened to September 1950 over 100 children aged five to eleven passed through it. Some were obviously too young to have given trouble, but of the others no more than five were known delinquents, in the sense that they have been 'picked up' by the police, and all five are from unsatisfactory homes. In addition three children from apparently good homes have stolen, but have not come under police notice. One is Terence whose story has already been told. Another is Arthur, whose mother would not buy him a torch. He took a pound note from inside her rent book and bought it himself. He came to school with a new torch, of which he was very proud, and a pocket full of silver—about fifteen shillings—which he gave away to all and sundry. This I believe to be purely infantile stealing, in which there is no sense of the value of money involved. It simply arises from an immature social outlook, and a lack of understanding of the laws of ownership. A good deal of that type of pilfering goes on in school among the younger children. A few beads or a knob of plasticine are slipped into a pocket. I think no real moral issue is involved, at this stage, although recognition of moral laws can gradually be brought out of it. The tragedy is that Arthur might have found himself a 'delinquent', except for the accident that the money came from his own home instead of from elsewhere. The third of these children was an emotionally disturbed girl who stole small sums from home, and has been recommended for child guidance.

In going through my list of children, I can pick out at least twenty-four children who are unstable or difficult and who might well have been delinquents except for the care and supervision given by their parents. It seems certain then that the problem of delinquency is primarily the responsibility of the parents. Where the home situation is good, delinquency rarely occurs, except occasionally as a neurotic symptom, and if it does occur, it is dealt with immediately by the parents in co-operation with the school.

Where the home is unsatisfactory, however, these children are most likely to drift into trouble, less through malice than through inefficiency in withstanding environmental influences, and in dealing with their own impulses. Since the parents of these children do not accept their responsibility, it is necessary that some form of supervision after school and at the week-ends should be introduced. This could best be done by play centres or junior clubs specially organized for mentally handicapped children since these do not always find a very happy place among more intelligent children.[1] It must be emphasized, however, that it would be the greatest mistake to encourage those children from satisfactory homes to join such clubs. If the parents can and will give supervision and control, and if they will take an interest in their children and help them to achieve stability, there can be nothing better. Such homes will give the children more than the best of clubs can even attempt to give, and these handicapped children will thrive best in the security of their parents' protective love.

The following case study shows how a child may drift towards delinquency for want of suitable occupation and supervision after school. His parents are willing but inadequate to help him.

[1] Local Education Authorities are not always very willing to co-operate in the formation of such clubs, nor sympathetic to the idea of using clubs in the prevention of delinquency. It would seem that some would prefer to spend money on supporting habitual delinquents in residential schools rather than to spend a little in providing a counter-attraction to crime.

JACK.

Mental age, 6 years 6 months.
Chronological age, 10 years 6 months.
I.Q. 62.

Attainments.

Reading age (Burt), 6 years 4 months.
Mental arithmetic age (Burt), 5 years 6 months.

Home Situation. Family lives in tiny top floor flat in a slum. Home not too clean, and not very comfortable from adult viewpoint, but baby (aged two) has toys all over floor, and it is a place where a child may make a mess (if he can find room to squeeze in at all). The kitchen is the living-room, and the other three tiny rooms have to be used as bedrooms.

Father has not worked for two years (neurosis). Before the war he was constantly out of work, and I remember him as a very sullen man, who sat by the fire sulking most of the day and was very difficult indeed. He now is extremely thin and lined but looks much more cheerful. He greeted me very amiably, invited me in and gave me a cup of tea. This would not have happened in 1939.

Mother is fat, comfortable and apparently good tempered. She is now embarking on the *Daily Express* slimming campaign. During the time I have known her she has kept her children tidy, well shod and well clothed, and they have looked well nourished, but she had to struggle alone while her husband settled down to a sulky life by the fire. The husband and wife seem now to be on the best of terms, and the general atmosphere is pleasant and homely. Both take a very great interest and pride in Janet (aged two) who has congenital hip trouble, so that she cannot walk, but humps herself along the floor. They fetched her box of jigsaws so that she could show her ability. She was able to do the puzzles without any difficulty.

Siblings:

Ronald aged twenty-one. Was a mechanic till he was called up. Now abroad with the forces. Ronald was rather sulky and self-willed as a child, but apparently has turned out steady, pleasant and entirely satisfactory. He shows no desire to marry, although his parents would like him to do so, as their bedroom space is so very limited (four boys have to share a very small room, when all are at home).

George was one of the most sensitive and sweetest-tempered children one could imagine. He won an art scholarship, but had to leave art school at fourteen years old, as his father was not working. He became a coalman for a time, but did not stick at any job. Would sit indoors all day, accepting his meals but 'never opening his mouth'. (Frustration of creative urge? Or a 'chip off the old block'? He is very like his father in appearance.) George is now in the army. His interests are boxing and athletics—rather surprisingly.

Bob seemed intelligent as a child, but did not win a scholarship. Secondary modern school. Was a most pathetic-looking child—very much like our Jack—and when he was evacuated the villagers would often cheer him with an apple or a cake. Unknown to the villagers his pathetic looks veiled the world's worst boy! Neither his mother, nor anybody else, could do anything with him. As he grew older he became interested in school work, and was much better behaved. All three brothers had excellent school-leaving reports. I do regard Bob as rather unstable though. He used to attend my club, and I have never seen a boy (aged twelve to thirteen then) so beside himself with excitement as he was over the simplest game of bagatelle. The three brothers get on very well indeed.

Jack—E.S.N.

Jacqueline—a much longed for girl. The three boys had wanted a sister when Jack was born, having been much taken by a little girl cousin. They asked their mother to send Jack back and get a girl. They 'have no time for Jack'—partly, of course, on account of his dullness, and also, perhaps, because they were in the reception area during his babyhood. Jacqueline is bright, and she tries to help Jack.

Janet—aged two. Jack takes a great interest in her, and loves to feed her or take her out in her invalid chair.

Family attitude to Jack, the mentally handicapped child. Both parents adopt a very reasonable attitude. Jack's maternal uncle was mentally defective. He is now placed on a farm. Neither blames Jack, nor are they impatient with him, although his elder brothers 'have no time for him'. His mother thinks that if they would take him to museums, etc., it would help him, but they are not interested. Jigsaw puzzles and toys are provided in the home but Jack slips off with other boys and gets into trouble. Parents look out for him in the afternoon, but he gives them the slip and does not return till after 9 p.m. They then give him a meal, then, lately, have spanked him and put him to bed. They have been advised to give him no supper, but I strongly supported them in their contention that that is not a wise course. They sometimes refuse him cake or 'afters', but never the main meal. I emphasized that home *must* be an attractive place, or why return to it at all? Also that, if he knows he will get no food when he gets home, he will be tempted to steal from the baker's shop at the corner. I happen to know that he used to do this, as a small boy, when cakes were 'on coupons'. Suggested that they should make him responsible, for example, for getting the tea ready, or feeding Janet, so that there is a real need for him to be at home. The parents are intelligent and at once said that they saw that he should have some responsibility. The mother is wondering whether it would be wise to apply for a residential school, where he would get discipline and supervision until he is sixteen. If he stays at home, in that neighbourhood and among his present companions, she foresees endless trouble for him between now and the time he is sixteen with, possibly, juvenile court and remand homes, etc. There is no question in this family of rejecting Jack or of making him feel the odd man out. Both parents are anxious to do their best to help him to face life, and are only wondering what means to employ to this end.

Jack has already been in trouble with the police during one of his after-school jaunts. Apparently he pushed a child off her tricycle and went for a ride himself, since when the tricycle has not been found. No charge was made, but Jack was questioned at the police station.

What chance has this child of getting through the remainder of his school life without delinquency?

Chapter V

SOCIAL TRAINING
IN THE SPECIAL SCHOOL

One of the most important functions of the school is to fit the child to take his place as a stable co-operative member of society. If he is to be a positive force for good, doing his part in leavening the whole, his life must be built on a love and reverence for what is good and true; and these sentiments must find expression in all his personal relationships. So the most important part of social training is the integration of the personality, so that the child is not left at the mercy of every momentary impulse, but is able to express, in his actions and relationships, sentiments and ideals which he has consciously accepted and made his own. Woven in with the development of the personality, is the achievement of social relations, first with the immediate family, then with the school, and then spreading out into the larger community into which he has been born. The personal life of the child or adult, and his relations with society are so welded together that one cannot be thought of apart from the other. Society is good just in so far as its members infuse goodness into it, and the good life, lived by a humble obscure member of a community is 'woven into the stuff of other men's lives'. If we are privileged to work with mentally handicapped children, we must realize their value as human personalities, we must have faith in their potentialities, as forces for good in society, and must believe that it is worth while to help them to achieve self-realization and stability. They will react to our belief in them, and will co-operate in the work we have set out to do, that of training them to become complete human beings and happy contributors to the well-being of their fellows. If we have not this belief in them, we must not attempt to work with these children at all.

Before the child comes to us, personal relationships have already been formed, with mother first, then father and then with the whole family. His relations with his family, and with himself when he is sufficiently mature to recognize himself as an individual, usually determine his attitudes to society and, in some cases, to the whole moral code. First in importance is the mother-child relationship. Does the mother give him love and security—or does he feel rejected? Does she coddle the backward child and make a baby of him when he should be feeling his way towards a measure of independence? Does she get impatient at his slowness and his apparent lack of response? Is his apathy taken for lack of reciprocal love? Is he allowed to make his little contribution where he can, or do his parents give favours while refusing to accept them? Does the father, or the whole family, begin to be ashamed of his dullness? Perhaps at three or four years old he cannot speak, can hardly walk, takes little interest, and sometimes the parents are disappointed, their pride is hurt, and they begin to compare him unfavourably with his brothers and sisters. However young, the child senses his parents' attitude, and as he begins to understand that he is not exactly what they had hoped for, he is discouraged, and feels inferior and rejected. Or, perhaps, before he is ready to stand upon his own feet, another baby arrives. He needs the protective love and security of his mother's full attention longer than a normal child, and he feels deprived when another baby usurps his place. Perhaps his brothers and sisters, or the other children in the street, tease him or jeer at him. At any rate, he with his slow development is soon left behind by his own age group, and he gradually takes it for granted that he can do nothing and that he has no place in the children's groups, even if he is allowed to feel that he has a place in the family group. When he goes to school, all this may be intensified. He cannot keep up, and would gladly retreat to the safety

SOCIAL TRAINING

of his mother's care. This cannot be, so he often retreats inside himself, and becomes withdrawn and aloof. He cannot find a place in the social group, so he simply withdraws from it. Left to develop on these lines, he will be unlikely to take any part in society at all, and will probably become unemployable and finally drift into an institution. On the other hand, the child who cannot keep up may become anti-social, attacking other children, becoming aggressive or even delinquent to compensate for his own inferiority.

So, when a child comes to a special school, there may be a great deal to undo, and a great many misapprehensions to break down, before the work of building an integrated personality and a co-operative social being can be started.

Very often this work of readjustment has to be carried out in very difficult material conditions. Many special school buildings are old-fashioned, and much in need of a bright coat of paint, playground space, etc. My own junior school has only sixty children between the ages of five and eleven, but the hall and playground are incredibly small, and the place is dingy and cramped. Visitors are often shocked by our building, but I contend that the spirit is more than material conditions, and that it is possible to build a community which is happy, co-operative, and welded together by a common tradition and a common purpose, however adverse the physical conditions may be. So long as each child is progressing slowly towards full and complete self-realization within his intellectual limitations, and is gradually reaching out towards co-operation with another child, with a group, or with adults, a poor building cannot discourage us.

Within the special school, we have to remember that a subnormal child may be very late in developing social habits and social play. He may need to be allowed weeks, months, or even years of individual experiment and activity before his social sense begins to develop. We must be careful not to force him into group play or group activities until he himself shows readiness. During this time his relations with his teacher are of the utmost importance. If his parents' reactions to him are unsatisfactory, it is his teacher who will give him that protective interest which will rebuild his sense of security, while, at the same time, she will try to get to know his parents and develop their interest in the child. If the child has been over 'babied' it is the teacher who will gradually lead him towards a greater independence. Re-educating the parents in this case is more difficult, for there must be no sudden reaction, no sharp break in their treatment of him, to bewilder him, to make him feel his inability to cope, or to make him feel deprived of love. Bobby was an only child of eight years old who had been kept too dependent by his mother. He was pale, timid, fastidious and slow in eating, and generally unable to look after himself. At seven, although his I.Q. appeared to be only 42, he was given a trial in a Special School. In the admission class he showed great timidity together with a secret spitefulness. He was very fond of drawing and showed considerable powers of observation. He was solitary and showed no interest in social relationships. At eight his I.Q. appeared to be 60[1] but he was more babyish than ever. He would ask his teacher to feed him with his dinner, would say he was unable to change his own shoes, put on his coat, etc. His mother was sent for, and she admitted that she was accustomed to doing all these things for him, but that, as she was at last expecting another baby she was, on the advice of her doctor, trying to wean him from this dependence. Here, we felt, lay a very great danger. That Bobby was feeling rejected and deprived of love was apparent in his regression in school. It was necessary that he should become more independent, but, we explained to his mother, this training in independence must not seem to be connected with the coming of the new baby, nor must it be so sudden that the child was

[1] At the age of eleven, Bobbie has gone to a secondary modern school, as his I.Q. is now over 80.

hurt and bewildered. His mother had told him of the new baby and had prepared him as well as possible, and he was looking forward to the event. We felt that it was quite the wrong moment for a change in his mother's attitude, and suggested that she should treat him as she had always done (bad though that had been for him) while we, at school, tried to train him in independence and self-reliance. She could then get him occasionally to do oddments for himself 'to help her', without letting him feel any break which could be interpreted as lack of love. This compromise worked well, as far as we can tell, and his mother, by now, has managed to wean him from his babyish attitude while maintaining an obvious love for him and an interest in all he does. So he has managed to achieve a reasonable independence without apparently feeling any sense of rejection. In cases where the parent is less co-operative and intelligent, a greater weight rests upon the school and teacher.

The social training of the child in school will begin then with the teacher-child relationship, and the establishment of confidence between them. If this is to be done, it is obvious that the teacher's role will not be to marshal the children, to bark out orders, nor to stand in front lecturing to them and directing them. Her part will rather be to encourage and help them to direct themselves. She will not require them to sit still and be silent, since she wishes to encourage social relationships, confidence, and security. It is quite obvious that there must be much freedom of movement, freedom to offer or invite co-operation with one another, and freedom to talk with one another or with the teacher. If we are to get the best from our junior sub-normals we must be prepared to use what are often called 'activity methods', even though they need to be modified to suit the mentality of the children we are dealing with. Because these children have comparatively little ability to control their immediate impulses, unmodified freedom might well lead to anti-social acts rather than to social co-operation. It is necessary therefore to protect the children from their own impulses and from those of others by a firm external control. This the teacher must supply in individual cases, lessening external control as the child develops self-control but ready always to 'take over' when a child's self-control breaks down. Unstable as most of these children are, there may be occasions all through their life when they will need strength from outside themselves to save them from their own weakness.

In the junior special school the admission class can best be run entirely as a nursery class. The mental ages in this class will all be under five years even though the actual ages may be from five to seven years. No formal work should be attempted here. To try to get children with mental ages of two and a half to four and a half years to do writing, reading or number is a sheer waste of very valuable time and a form of cruelty which lays up trouble for the future. They need every opportunity for activity and experiment with real materials—water and sand play, house play, dolls, large and small wheeled toys, etc. They may wish to play alone, but even so they learn to take turns with toys, and to acknowledge the prior claim of another to the toy both want. Many opportunities for social play with toys arise quite spontaneously. For example, the see-saw is only possible if two children co-operate. Educational apparatus is used as in a nursery school, and there is painting, using large sheets of paper and big brushes, for individual self-expression, while the nesting bridge and slide, together with much of the other apparatus, encourages, without demanding, group co-operation. The training involved in sharing toys, in putting apparatus away tidily, in using all materials carefully does not need to be emphasized. Keeping the classroom tidy, helping with the nature table, painting pictures to decorate the wall—all help in developing a sense of service to the little community, which, if fostered, should lead later to good and loyal membership of school, family and society.

SOCIAL TRAINING

Outside, the children have sometimes been exploited by other children on account of their disability, but here they find that might is *not* necessarily right, and that no stronger child is allowed to interfere with them. So their sense of security is strengthened. Group activities should be introduced, for example, news, discussions, stories, music and movement, etc., but a child who is not ready for these should be left with the nursery assistant, while those who are sufficiently developed socially enjoy such activities. To force group activity before a child is ready for social co-operation is to undermine the whole of the social training we hope to give. Social life must be built on a voluntary basis. It is held together by love and co-operation, and neither of these can be forced. Unless our foundations are strong we can build nothing which will last. Good solid foundations are worth waiting for. Leave the child to develop naturally, and he will find out for himself the value of social relationships. Force him into social life and he will become a misfit.

Speech is, perhaps, the most valuable social medium we have. In these children, speech often develops very late, and I am inclined to think that the development of social readiness lags behind until the child begins to speak. I have certainly noticed that older children who cannot speak, or who are almost unintelligible, are easily exasperated, spiteful and anti-social. As speech improves these habits tend to disappear. A most important part of the educational and social training all through the school, is done in the field of language. Conversations with one another or with the teacher, news and stories, dramatisation, mime, puppets—in fact as much talking as possible is necessary, in order that the child may learn to communicate his thoughts, feelings and desires to other people. To develop the power of self-expression through speech is one of the basic needs of these children, and it is a power which they are rarely able to develop normally, unless a great deal of help is given, together with very frequent opportunities to talk to one another in school, not only in the playground.) Expression through speech is helped considerably by much self-expression through other media—painting, clay modelling, mime, etc. These are especially useful in the case of withdrawn children. As the children go about their own work, singly or in groups, learning, under the influence of the teacher, to show courtesy and consideration for others, and practising speech for the natural and right reason, the desire or need to communicate with others (and not because the teacher requires a sentence about this or that!), they are taking their place in their own community, and are training for social co-operation in the larger world of adult life.

Betty, aged six, came to us having been excluded from an Infant School because she would neither speak nor move. She had to be lifted from her seat and carried bodily to the playground, and she had never been known to speak in school, though she was said to chatter at home. We did not worry her to speak or to join in activities, but let her play alone as long as she wished. Gradually she began to talk, first to her teacher and then to the other children. She loved singing and was ready to sing alone within two years. She had shown spiteful habits which disappeared as speech developed, and now, after three years in a junior E.S.N. school, she is lively, happy and even cheeky. She has no difficulty in talking, except with strangers, when she appears too shy to speak. She has, however, difficulty with pronouncing some consonants, and, in view of her history we think this may be of emotional origin. It seems advisable to let her gain full confidence before this speech defect as such is tackled, although she has been recommended for Child Guidance.[1]

If a child is to be acceptable to society, he must learn how things are done in his community, and how to achieve personal

[1] Betty is now ten, and will speak even to strangers, is beginning to read and takes an interest in number. In the music and mime she will act freely and speak spontaneously even before a crowd of visitors.

SOCIAL TRAINING

cleanliness and good manners. These things help to build up his self-respect, so that he is able to take his place naturally and without undue feelings of inferiority. A dull child is doubly handicapped if he is uncouth, awkward, and ill-mannered. So the admission class children must spend a good proportion of the time in learning to put on coats, do up buttons, change shoes, wash themselves and do their own hair, and keep their noses clean. Often the mothers have found it quicker to wait on these children than to teach them to wait on themselves—so again the school helps to make up for the lack of suitable home training. The children get their little beds ready for their afternoon sleep, set their tables for dinner, learn how to use a knife and fork, wipe the cloths clean after the meal. They have a real sense of achievement when they are able to do small things for themselves, and their pride in their new-found abilities is encouraging to us as well as to them. This training in personal hygiene and social manners must continue throughout school life.

The development together of self-respect, confidence, social poise, and ability to cope with personal hygiene, is illustrated by the study of an older E.S.N. girl between the ages of thirteen and sixteen. At thirteen Grace was a hoyden, who could do nothing. She had been in London while the schools were closed and had received little or no training in social habits and cleanliness. Then we visited the homes and got these children into school. Grace responded very quickly to the educational and social training. Her ability was very slight, and her I.Q. low, but her work was beautifully clean and neat. Personal hygiene was the real difficulty. Again and again she was found dirty, and she was so persistently verminous that the Health Visitor went to inspect her home. This was found to be clean, but her mother expressed the very common belief that 'some kids breed 'em'. In the meantime, Grace was becoming a leader among the other girls. Between the ages of fourteen and fifteen she surprised us all by her stability and common sense, as well as by her qualities of leadership. Her chief weakness was a habit of sulking. She got a group together to practise plays, which they performed to entertain us all, and generally she seemed socially able. Yet she remained dirty. One day I let her be headmistress of the school, and she chose her staff from the most stable of the girls, and set them up in their classrooms. There were no disorderly lines that day! Grace was in and out of the classrooms to see what staff and children were about, and she knew exactly how each class was being conducted and what work was being done. I put on my hat and announced myself as an inspector, and she received me perfectly—shaking hands, and conducting me round the classes with far more poise and self-confidence than I feel in a similar situation! At midday I found that her meal was laid in my room—and after dinner she demanded a cup of tea! All this confidence and poise deserted her when some children brought her to my evening club for normal children. She neither moved nor spoke, and when she was chosen for 'blind man' she stood still and made not the feeblest attempt to catch anybody. She needed her 'prepared environment' at that stage, but the way she carried over her sense of responsibility into ordinary life later on astonished us.

The school Sister had a talk with her, when she was about fourteen and a half years old, and asked her to try to get clean. She set to work at home, and by herself, without any help, managed to get her head clean before the next inspection. From that time till she left school at sixteen years she had a clean head. At the same time she began to wash and iron her own clothes, and they were beautifully kept. She was very undersized and undeveloped—more like a child of eleven years, and she had a very white skin and straight fair hair. Her ankle socks were white and clean, and her clothing beautifully washed and ironed and fresh. She looked more like a little princess in a fairy tale, than the dirty untidy child who had first come to us. I regard the whole transformation as due to

SOCIAL TRAINING

the interaction of confidence, social training, the development of self-respect and independence, and the need for being accepted by her community. Such stability did this child acquire that she has kept one job (in a factory) ever since leaving school five years ago.

The midday meal is a grand opportunity for social training. The children have jobs to do—setting tables, pouring out water, etc., which help to build up their self-respect and their sense of responsibility. In our school each teacher has volunteered to have her meal with her own class. Her table faces the children's tables, and all are set with bright cloths, and flowers when these are obtainable. It is very rare for any comment to be made upon table manners by the teacher, but the children learn by following her example, and an immense improvement has been made. It is very rare now to see a child, unless it be a newcomer, eating a potato as if it were a toffee apple. During the meal the children talk together or with the teacher, and the whole atmosphere is that of a family meal. After the meal the children wipe the cloths and get the room ready for the afternoon.

If children are admitted at the age of five to six years a comparatively clear start in social training can be made in the admission class, but when they are admitted later there is often a great deal to contend with. Home training has not been supplemented by the individual care which we are able to give in our very small admission classes. Habits of slovenly behaviour have become stronger, self-respect has been dulled by the feeling of inferiority, and a suspicious attitude to other people may have developed. They have been failing consistently in the ordinary school, always in their work and usually in their social relationships. They are deeply discouraged, and their feeling of inferiority is shown often in some form of behaviour disorder, or in their withdrawn and apathetic attitude. Some more extreme cases are discussed in the section on 'Misfits in the Special E.S.N. School'. The ordinary late-comer usually settles down fairly well when he finds that he is no longer the 'dunce', that the work is fitted to him, and that he can go at his own pace and, most important of all, that we appreciate his efforts, his achievements and his personality. The most heartening discovery such a child can make is that he is acceptable, first to the adults, and then to the children in his community. Social training is, however, a slower and less sure process with these late-comers, for they have already learned to be suspicious of others, and it is much more difficult to get their trust and co-operation. Gradually it is built up, but we have to be very patient during the process. The small classes, the individual interest and attention, and the special methods help to restore the child's confidence in himself and in adults. He has probably become self-seeking by the time he comes to us, but freedom from competition helps to allay his suspicions of the other children, so that the first step has been taken towards co-opera- in place of competition, and consideration for others in place of self-seeking.

I may quote here the case of Rose. Rose, aged nine years, had been in residential E.S.N. schools, as far as we could gather, from the age of five and a half. Little of her past history was available, but she was still at a residential school while attending a day special school. We were asked by her former day school to take her, as she had been quite unmanageable, and had ended by slapping the face of the attendant. When she came to us she was like a wild thing. She was very strongly built, very rough and loud-voiced, she shouted and laughed loudly, and her whole attitude was of resentment and rebellion. She would run about the room, snatch things from the teacher's table, hit children or destroy their work, and on Friday afternoon she finished up by dancing on the teacher's table wearing her gloves. In addition to this there were complaints of indecent behaviour in the playground and insolence to any adult who spoke to her. Her case can only be summarized briefly here, but the main points were:

SOCIAL TRAINING

1. To break down her resentment and fear of authority we humoured her for a while, simply distracting her attention when she was 'awkward'.

2. To protect the other children from her rough, spiteful and indecent behaviour, she was invited—as a treat—to spend her play times in the head teacher's room, choosing her own occupations or talking things out as she wished.

3. As far as possible we ignored her completely when she was 'showing off' by being rough or insolent, but talked with her quietly when she was in a good mood, telling her how glad we were to have her, how much we liked her and how sorry we would be to lose her. When this had been assimilated and she wanted to become one of us, we began to put new ideals before her, showing her how impossible life would be if everybody behaved roughly and rudely and demanded the best of everything. We explained how very much more we would appreciate her if she did not always want her own way, but could join in and co-operate with us. Rose was a borderline case and was intelligent enough to understand this reasoning.

Our greatest help in this case was the attitude of the other children. They looked on Rose as rather a nuisance, not as a heroine, and only once did we have a child attempting to join in Rose's rebellion. Rose gradually assimilated the new ideas we were trying to give her, together with the standards of conduct shown by the other children. She wanted to 'belong' —it was the greatest need of her life, a need which, I believe, was at the bottom of all her anti-social behaviour. She put all the strength of her nature into trying to achieve her new ideal, so that in only six months this note was added to her record sheet:

'Rose shows steady improvement with very occasional lapses. Her voice is normally quiet, she rarely answers back, and, on the whole, is co-operative and sensible. She is most anxious to get on in her work. Her teacher says that she is no trouble in class, but is quietly helpful, and very interested and hard-working.'

This result had been achieved by allaying the child's suspicions of teachers and children, by long suffering and patience, but above all by the readiness of the whole community to accept the newcomer as she was, to believe in her so that she trusted us and was encouraged to work to her capacity and to assimilate a new ideal of living. She, like the other late-comers, began to desire to be one of this new community in which she found herself, rather than to make herself an outsider. The realization that nobody can make a child an outsider but himself, that all depends upon himself, and that social failure is not attributable to the attitude of others, is the greatest step forward.

Usually the child will volunteer for jobs, and helping to clean and feed the pets, giving out the milk, collecting the empty bottles, and other odd jobs, however small, help to build up an ideal of service. At the same time he feels that he really is accepted, now that he is singled out to do such jobs. Thus we try to uproot the earlier sense of failure and suspicion, and to lay a new foundation of confidence, trust and loyalty on which social co-operation may be built.

It is necessary throughout the school to have much free activity, in which the child can experiment with his new values, play out his problems, and express himself as fully as possible. At the same time, for the older children, social activities should also be organized—games, singing, mime, dancing, dramatic work, group reading and number activities, gardening, group discussions, educational visits. In these he will learn to give and take, to lead and to submit, so satisfying some of his deepest needs. He will gradually develop generosity to others, loyalty to his group, and self-reliance within an organized unit, all of which are indispensable to life in any community. Through all this he should finally form a truer picture of himself and his

SOCIAL TRAINING

place in society. Slowly he learns how to satisfy all his legitimates desires and how to sublimate those which are not socially acceptable (see section on 'Misfits').

Naturally he does not go forward without relapses. It is necessary to have some way of dealing with these, and also with deliberate naughtiness, which is part of every child's equipment. In my school, as far as possible we try to work on social lines. We emphasize that every child who is present (or *legitimately* absent) and who is behaving as an ordinary, hard-working, co-operative member of his group, is giving active honour to his school. The school is proud of such members, and their names are on our 'Honours Board'. This has nothing to do with the ability to read, etc. It is only concerned with the will to do what is right. There the name stays, showing the whole world that its owner is a credit to us all, until some anti-social behaviour occurs. Then the child is requested to remove his name from the board, and to take it to the head teacher, who keeps it until he has 'won it back'. As soon as he merits it, he fetches his name and puts it back on the Honours Board. The name is never, of course, removed for failure in any kind of school work, but only for anti-social behaviour. We have found this very effective in that it emphasizes the value of ordinary everyday effort rather than that of innate ability, there is no element of competition in it, the unacceptable behaviour has an *immediate* result in the removal of the name and the consequent lowering of status, and while the name, status, and honour can be restored only by the efforts of the child himself, it *can* be restored very quickly. There is no carry over from week to week, but every name appears on the Honours Board every Monday morning.

Throughout our work in social training one rather difficult adjustment has to be made—that between actual age, emotional age and mental age. The discrepancy between these may be considerable. As with all our other problems, this can only be considered in relation to the individual child, but on the whole

I think it is true to say that while their work must be based upon their mental age, their behaviour should correspond more nearly to their actual age, unless there is definite emotional retardation. It is useless to teach children of ten with a mental age of five to read. But a child of ten who acts like a child of five is doubly handicapped. In most cases, a child can be helped to conduct himself more nearly in accordance with his actual age, because, although mentally younger, he has had the physical experience of children of his own age. To make babies of children because their mental age is low, is to make them unacceptable in the larger world outside the school. So we are wise, I think, to expect a degree of controlled behaviour comparable to that expected in the bottom classes of an ordinary junior school, i.e. ages seven and eight, but, at the same time, we must be ready to compensate for what the child lacks in self-control so that he can accomplish this without strain. By this I mean that we must be willing to exert control when necessary, we must not talk down to the children, we must give them reasons for the rules we make, we must discuss things with them and get to know their own point of view. Giving reasons and discussing with them may not at first sight appear very fruitful, as their mental age is so low and these are mental processes, but I think that the attempt is well worth while. As far as conduct is concerned, I think that a child, for example nine years of age, with a mental age of five years, should not be expected to rush about indoors shouting, but should learn to walk and use 'indoor manners'. He should be able to act in an orderly manner, not pushing and shoving, but recognizing that other people have a right to consideration. He should be expected at times to settle to a task, even if he has not himself chosen it, and to carry it through, even though the impulse may be to discard it for a more attractive job. By the top end of the junior E.S.N. school the child—even with the mental age of a child in the lower infant school—should understand that he cannot always expect immediate attention and that he must not interrupt if his teacher is attending to some other matter. Controlled conduct may not be in accordance with a nursery or lower infant school mental age, but my experience has been that it is better for the child to learn how to conduct himself in the world outside, than to find himself a butt for the ridicule of his own age group, and the child of whom his family is ashamed. This standard of social behaviour will not prove too great a strain for the child, provided that he is allowed a very great deal of free play and creative activity, in which his infantile mentality and emotional impulses can find expression, and provided that his school work is carefully fitted to his mental development. We have always to remember that while children are selected for special schools on an educational and intellectual basis, at the age of sixteen a social criterion is employed. At sixteen these children have to take their place in normal society. On their normal standard of behaviour, and not on their ability to read and write, their success in life depends. They may leave school with a mental age of seven or eight years,[1] but if we have helped them to make the adjustment between their seven-year-old abilities and their sixteen-year-old physique, giving them hobbies and outlets for their seven-year-old reactions, and a poise and control which more nearly approaches a sixteen-year-old standard, they should, with continued help and supervision, be able to take their place fairly well among the normal adolescents who are more highly endowed intellectually. Provided that this general atmosphere of controlled freedom is maintained, a school develops a tradition and spirit of its own. This is quickly absorbed even by late admissions, and they, with the already established members, are bound into a community with a common life and purpose.

We have emphasized the need for personal expression, and the development of social co-operation and now we come to the need for some form in which the community as a whole can

[1] At the age of sixteen years a mental age of $7\frac{6}{12}$ gives I.Q. 50.

express itself. Generally, I think, this opportunity is best afforded by the morning assembly and the corporate act of worship. This is the business of the children themselves, and they should be helped to make it their own. Their skill in reading, speaking, singing, etc., their ability to lead and their willingness to follow should all be used in this one corporate effort. In my own school we usually take a daily central idea, for example The Good Shepherd, on which hymns, readings and prayers are based. Every morning three or four children volunteer to lead the prayers, and one or two good readers are chosen also. We begin with a Good Shepherd hymn. Then the children sit while a child reads, from a huge family Bible we found in the cupboard, a passage such as 'The Lord is my Shepherd' or 'I am the good Shepherd'. This passage is discussed, then a second Good Shepherd hymn is sung. The leaders then make up prayers, for example, 'Thank you God for taking care of us', while the others answer 'Thank you God'. A second reading usually follows, and then a last hymn. Sometimes we use mime at the morning assembly. For example, the story of the Annunciation is told, and then mimed freely by the children. Appropriate hymns are sung, and passages from the Bible are read by the children. On another day we have the spontaneous dramatization of another story . . . the arrival at the inn, the shepherds, the angels, the three kings . . . and finally all the stories are mimed as one story, the scenes being divided by readings and hymns, the whole ending with the children's own extempore prayers. Hymns usually are one verse only, the prayers, readings, and discussion are very short, so that attention does not flag. It is my belief that, in addition to its religious significance, this morning assembly is one of the best means of social training we possess.

There remains to consider those children who do not settle down well even in the special school. These are the withdrawn children, who fail to develop a normal attitude of social co-operation, the aggressive and uncontrolled children who

SOCIAL TRAINING

appear definitely anti-social, and the unstable children who are completely unreliable and who form a very difficult social problem. These are discussed more fully in the section 'Misfits in the Special E.S.N. School', while delinquency has already been discussed under its own heading.

Chapter VI
MISFITS IN THE SPECIAL E.S.N. SCHOOL
EXPERIMENTS IN THE TREATMENT OF MALADJUSTMENT IN EDUCATIONALLY SUB-NORMAL CHILDREN
(I.Q.'S 45 TO 75)

The life of a normal person is a constant series of adjustments and readjustments. The more nearly an individual approaches to true normality and balance, the more easily these adjustments are made. The person who is handicapped by mental deficiency, by psychopathic, neurotic or other abnormal tendencies, or by psychoneuroses developed through early environmental conditions, may appear unable to adjust himself, and so becomes a social misfit, or 'maladjusted'.

Psychopathic conditions are the concern of specialists in mental disease; and we, as teachers, have little to do with their prevention or treatment.

Neuroses and behaviour disorders in children of normal intelligence are, at the present time, receiving considerable attention from social workers, parents and teachers co-operating under the direction of psychiatrists. Many more cases are awaiting treatment than the hospitals and child guidance clinics can possibly cope with. While this condition persists, it is almost impossible to get psychiatric treatment for maladjusted children of sub-normal intelligence (I.Q.'s 45 to 75). Moreover, children whose I.Q.'s are below 75 are usually less responsive to psychiatric treatment than those of more normal intelligence and simpler methods of treatment are often more appropriate. It is, therefore, inevitable that psychiatric treatment should usually be given chiefly in those cases where the prognosis is more hopeful. Where behaviour disorders and inability to cope with life in E.S.N. children have been noted, these conditions have usually been regarded as inherent in mental handicap, and segregation in a special school has been considered a sufficient remedy, or at least a sufficient palliative.

Special School Treatment

Many children of sub-normal intelligence, who have been misfits in an ordinary school, do, in fact, settle down almost immediately in a special school. In small classes where individual attention can be given, among other children who are similarly handicapped, and in an environment especially prepared for their education, they are usually able to adjust themselves without any difficulty. Their former difficulties were largely due to the fact that their psychological development lags behind that of other children of their age. The work and social activities of their class have been beyond them, so that they have developed a sense of inferiority and a habit of idleness, followed often by mischievous and unruly behaviour, sometimes by delinquency and in some cases by withdrawal. They have always been the 'dunce' of the class, and the shame of their family, so they have become fearful of attempting any piece of work, since bitter experience has taught them that it is almost bound to fail. If this state of things goes on for too long, their innate abilities appear almost to atrophy. For example, a girl who was due to leave an ordinary school in six months' time was referred by the School Medical Officer[1] for statutory examination. Among her papers was a letter from her headmistress. She was, she said, outraged that Sheila should be examined. She had never recommended a child for 'one of those schools', except in the case of one boy who was dangerous, and another who had 'very nasty habits'. In her opinion Sheila was not more than seriously retarded. The doctor attempted to test Sheila, but after years of being the 'dunce' of

[1] Her extreme dullness was noticed by the doctor at the physical examination, and steps were taken to have her examined.

her school, she was afraid to venture any answer. At each question she burst into frightened sobs. After much patient work the doctor succeeded in winning her confidence, and was able to test. The result was an I.Q. of only 40—too low even for a special school! Yet there is little doubt in my mind that Sheila's innate intelligence was higher than appeared, but that years of unsympathetic treatment in an ordinary school had paralysed her capabilities, and spoiled her hopes of succeeding in life. In such a case as this, special school treatment *at an early age* would probably have afforded all the help Sheila needed in establishing an integrated personality although on a low intelligence level. In the ordinary school Sheila's reaction was to become timorous, quiet and apathetic, but if, on the contrary she had developed obvious behaviour disorders—insolence, unruliness, stealing, sex precocity or delinquency of any kind—she would probably have found her way to a special school, following the boy 'who was dangerous', and the one 'who had very nasty habits'.

In the special school our first task is to restore the child's confidence, to find some activity he can 'shine' in, so that he can gradually lose his aversion to school and his fear of failure. This aversion to school causes hysterical illnesses and truancy, and only a sense of achievement in school can combat it. One girl admitted at thirteen, who was most irregular in attendance, changed her whole outlook when she was allowed to polish the floor of my little room instead of doing reading and number. She could, at last, be a useful member of the community instead of a 'dunce'. Another (who left us at sixteen years with an I.Q. of 37, and who has kept one steady job in a laundry ever since, i.e. five years) found her niche in doing odd jobs—even clearing up when a little one was sick. We applauded good work of *all* kinds—reading and number took its place as equal *but not superior* to odd jobs and polishing. Even in practical work and odd jobs these children need constant and patient supervision. If they remained in an ordinary school these 'jobs' would almost certainly be given to A stream children, who are better, quicker and more efficient even at routine tasks.

Other children come to us with really frightening school records—'Attacks other children, and is abusive, spiteful and uncontrollable.'—'subject to brain-storms, when he screams and kicks and is quite unmanageable. No member of this staff has been able to control him.' The boy who arrived with this last reputation had obviously been teased and set upon by other boys until he was beyond himself. He looked sub-normal (many of our children look quite normal) and children will often tease and bully such children, especially if they can hope to work them up into a show of fury. From the day he entered special school he gave no hint of trouble, except that he was rather suspicious of the other children, would sometimes give them a sly pinch, and was inclined to tell tales. Apart from this he was pleasant, co-operative and obedient. There is, then, some justification for the belief that special school treatment is a sufficient solution of the problem of these children. This, however, is not the whole picture.

Misfits among Sub-normal Children

There are cases where early environmental conditions and continuing undesirable influences have made so deep an impression that the child finds it almost impossible to settle down and co-operate fully, even in a special school. It is my belief that *some* of these children have a far higher intelligence than appears from the tests given in their statutory examination, but that their abilities are so paralysed by their psychological condition that they are unable to use them fully. In some cases, for example that of Ronald, the I.Q. appeared to be as low as 45, and yet, with the experimental treatment we gave, there was almost always a tendency for the I.Q. to *appear* to rise, and in Ronald's case it rose to 89,[1] thus qualifying him for

[1] Six boys aged ten to eleven years have recently been 'deascertained' (September 1952). All were emotionally disturbed children with apparently ascending I.Q.'s. Four more are awaiting 'deascertainment'.

deascertainment. The apparent improvement in I.Q. is purely incidental, and is in no sense the aim of this experiment. If the I.Q. appeared to go down, it would be no argument against these methods, provided the child became a co-operative member of a group and a happier child.

I.Q.'s appear to rise in many cases which were not included in this experiment, and for a variety of reasons. For example, a 'bone-lazy' child—too indolent even to play with a toy—showed a marked improvement in I.Q. when in the class of a strict disciplinarian of the old school, who insisted upon his working. There is no doubt that individual cases need individual treatment, and our experimental freedom might need, in one case, to be altered to strict control, or to be modified in some lesser way. The whole thing must be in accordance with the needs of the individual child.

If a child really has a potential intelligence of above 75, it is obvious that special E.S.N. school treatment, as generally understood, is bound to fail. The child was a fish out of water in an ordinary school because psychological difficulties kept him from *using* his potentialities, but he is equally a fish out of water among the mentally handicapped.

Whether these children are really neurotic, whether the tendencies we notice are reaction character traits or merely abnormal developments of simple character traits, is not for a teacher to diagnose. As we are usually unable to get a psychiatrist interested in apparently sub-normal cases, we have to observe what we can and experiment with such treatment as appears useful in alleviating the surface condition, hoping and praying that the cause may be dealt with in the process. In some cases we imagine we may have guessed at the cause, in other cases it remains buried too deeply for us to reach.

Maturation

The mental development of E.S.N. children is slower than that of more intelligent children, and they are continually

MISFITS IN THE SPECIAL E.S.N. SCHOOL

failing to catch up with life. Unfortunately, in the home and in the ordinary school, there is little understanding of, or patience with, this unreadiness to reach the usual stage at the usual age. Social play, social life and social responsibilities are forced upon them long before they are ready, and they are rather in the position of one who has caught the handrail of a moving bus, and can neither let go nor get on, but runs behind, lagging more and more—getting dragged for a while—then, either somebody stops the bus, or the would-be passenger manages to let go. The situation is an uncomfortable and dangerous one, and one in which steady development of the child's potentialities is impossible. The dependent period of babyhood needs to be prolonged for them. They need the exclusive care and attention of their mother long after they are ousted by the arrival of the next baby. Although the mother of a sub-normal child can do much harm by 'babying' him too long, yet the deprivation of the protective love which they need so much can do even more harm.

The Period of Solitary Play and Experiment

These children need a longer period when they are free to play and experiment in solitude and freedom. Often at, and beyond, seven years old, they are quite unready to co-operate with either children or adults. No doubt they are forced, both in their homes and in ordinary schools, to join in social games and activities long before they are ready to do so spontaneously, and so the seeds of social conflict are sown. Human contact begins to fret them. Adults are constantly breaking in upon their privacy (or solitude—the little world in which they are free to experiment and to 'figure things out') giving orders to which they feel unable to respond, or nagging them for failures which they cannot help. They are not allowed to grow in secrecy and aloneness, the world around them becomes more incomprehensible and more distasteful. Children are always round them, asking co-operation which they are unready to give, teasing, bullying or 'babying' them, or they are having to take the responsibility of minding younger children long before they are capable of independence and practical initiative. It is not surprising that such children should withdraw from such an unsympathetic world and live almost entirely in one of their own devising. So they do not hear when spoken to, appear blank, expressionless and without emotions. Their blankness is the guardian of their solitude, their lack of outward emotion simply shows the degree of their withdrawal into another world where there is no interference. Their lack of the emotions of pleasure, pain, or love may be compared with the power of primitive peoples, e.g. Red Indians to dissociate themselves from pain, and so become more stoical. The pain of repulsed love in early childhood may cause this emotionless attitude—a refusal to be hurt again. It will be noted that, in our experiments with these children, we found that periods of solitude, not *loneliness*, varying in length according to the needs of the child, was one of the most efficacious means of readjusting them to social life. (See case notes.)

Speech

Linked up with the problem of maturation in social contacts, is the problem of late-developing speech, and persistent speech defects. Speech usually develops late in E.S.N. children. In 1949 and 1950 I investigated the case papers of thirty-seven and forty-three children respectively. In both groups I found that the average age at which the child began to speak (i.e. simplest words) was round about four years old. Out of the forty-three cases in 1950, four children were not yet beginning to speak at the age of seven, and six were only just beginning at the age of six. It is not surprising that these children are unable to take a place in social life, since communication is almost always through speech. It is possible that speech and social abilities develop together, and that one cannot be very much in advance of the other. It is noticeable that children who retain bad speech defects—some remain almost unintelligible—are spiteful, easily exasperated, and annoying to other children, so that they tend to become the 'Ishmaels' even of a special school. This may happen even with a child like Brian, whose I.Q. was as high as 78. A speech therapy class in each special school is a crying need. Recently our L.E.A. has sent a speech therapist to assess the speech development in special schools, and we hope that some help will come from this.[1] In the meantime we do what we can, and especially we hope that our newly formed music and mime class will help gradually to develop the power of expression through spontaneous speech. (See notes on mime group.)

Types of apparent 'Maladjustment' among E.S.N. Special School Children

1. *The Withdrawn Type*

As a result of the unbearable pressure of the external world upon the slow-developing mentally handicapped child, some are driven inward, retreating from a life with which they cannot cope. These children are withdrawn, absent-minded, expressionless and apparently without affections or emotions. Their environment appears to make little impression upon them. Nothing seems to give them pleasure or pain, they show no enthusiasms, and make no friendships. For example, see the case notes of Fred Brown. Many others are repressed and withdrawn to a lesser degree. One of the strongest predisposing causes in such cases is, I believe, lack of a proper degree of solitude or privacy, together with a deprivation of protective love. These children give little trouble and are often left to their own devices. The anti-social type is far more likely to be dubbed maladjusted and to receive attention.

---

[1] We now have a visiting speech therapist who is doing excellent work with some very difficult cases.

2. Children with Behaviour Difficulties

Firstly there are the real delinquents—children who truant, steal, enter houses and open gas-meters, etc. For these children we can do little *directly*. We can help to give them moral standards, but the E.S.N. child faced with a concrete temptation is unlikely to be swayed by moral standards which belong to the realm of abstract thought. He may know right from wrong *in theory*. Yet even in the intellectually normal person the ideal sometimes seems less real than the concrete situation and so he acts in a way which he knows to be wrong (cf. St. Paul, 'The good that I would I do not . . .' etc.). This situation is intensified for the E.S.N. child and he needs more control from outside himself. It can hardly be hoped that he will ever achieve complete self-control. The problem of delinquency is primarily a problem for the parents, and teachers can achieve little, although they must adventure much. I sometimes think that complete supervision of E.S.N. children is the only real answer, for example, school till four, club till bedtime, then home and bed. A better provision would be enlightened parents, good homes with mother *at home* and not at work, high moral standards in the home, together with loving interest in the children—but who is to build this background? We have to deal with realities, not with ideal conditions.

The behaviour difficulties with which the school can and must deal, are resentment, defiance, insolence, disobedience, and anti-social tendencies within the school community, whether these are linked with anti-social acts out of school time or not. Resentment, with its attendant traits, obviously arises from unsuitable treatment, over-spoiling followed by harshness, sarcasm, contempt, lack of firmness, and, above all, lack of true affection and interest. In dealing with cases of this kind, we are brought up against the problem of punishment.

For the peace and security of the school as a body, children cannot be allowed to defy, to shout back answers, to swear at teachers, attendants or children, to slap the faces of other children without provocation, to destroy the work and interfere in the games of other children, to demand the best of everything 'or else——!' which is a very usual form of blackmail which they attempt to practise upon adults. We dare not allow all this—but the difficulty is to find a way of preventing it. We all know that the ideal is to reorient their energies, and to give them a new outlook. But this takes time, while the problem is urgent and immediate. These children are not yet interested in work, nor can they co-operate in play. While working on the right lines on a long-term policy, we cannot have the whole school outraged or corrupted by failing to find immediate measures. In dealing with the children we have to show a very real sympathy, and yet we must not do violence to their preconceived ideas of justice, nor outrage the sense of justice of the whole school. We must approve of and accept the child, but not what he does. Both the offender and the other children believe that such behaviour as has been described deserves punishment, whatever we adults may surmise as to the motivation in a particular case. Failure to deal strongly with an offender is taken as weakness by him, and is the cause of much resentment among the others. The result of this may be a ganging up of the other children to set upon the teacher's pet and punish him themselves, and children can be very cruel, or it may be that they will accept his leadership, imitate his ways, and gang up with him against authority. For the sake of the whole community we must restrain anti-social behaviour, and must punish offenders. But how is this to be done? The problem is a very real one. Generally such children are not yet amenable to moral suasion, nor to reasoned argument, although this must be tried. We have to recognize that it will be some time, however, before these means will be successful. In the meantime we can deprive a child of his little pleasures or his games—but what a privation that is! Not only does the child lose more enjoyment than we grown-ups can imagine, because his pleasures are so very vivid and his griefs are so very strong and he can imagine no future in which such grief can be forgotten, but he loses immeasurable opportunities of social adjustment when he cannot join in the pleasures and the games of his fellows. To keep him writing lines when he should be racing about, to nag or jaw him, or to use sarcasm is cruel and often has a disastrous effect upon the child's mind. I have come to the conclusion that, once we have gained a child's confidence, and he knows from experience that we will always give him a fair deal whatever the circumstances, it is better, when occasion demands, to give a slap, than to do violence to the children's preconceived sense of justice, on the one hand, or to use one of the other forms of punishment which seem so humane to adults and so cruel to children. There is also the consideration that, if he knows beforehand the penalty for certain offences, he may consider whether the adventure is worth while or not. If we remove the hazard by taking away all the penalties, he will be driven to seek adventure farther afield in such delinquency as attracts the attention of the police.

I have never found that a slap, given in cold blood without any sign of anger or exasperation, causes resentment or leads to lack of confidence. On the contrary, I have found that a child's sense of security is reinforced when he finds that one who has an obvious interest in and affection for him is strong enough to deal with him. The implication is that one is, therefore, strong enough to deal with his enemies. On the other hand, I am strongly of the opinion that corporal punishment, however light, should be the exception rather than the rule, and that it should be used only for certain offences which are well known to the children. All our children know that no penalty attaches to a fair fight between equals, but that ganging up to attack and beat up one child is rewarded by a slapping to each member of the gang, however many. Nothing could be more impersonal. In the same way, abusive language and behaviour is well known to merit a smack.

How are we to manage in the early stages, before we have

gained the confidence of a child? Social security demands his punishment, but I strongly disagree with giving a slap until full confidence is established. In such cases, I have found it better to remove the child from his class, and to let him stay in the head teacher's room for a few days in which he builds up confidence in her, than to risk punishing him, or alternatively to risk doing violence to the sense of justice of those children who have witnessed his offence. Having given the case for corporal punishment, as I see it, I may add that this is most rarely used in our school, and that every effort is made to rebuild preconceived ideas of justice, and to get the children to distinguish between what should be punished and what should be pitied and helped. In the case of Rose (described elsewhere) the children of her class really did co-operate with us, and seemed to reach a real understanding of her needs and limitations. It is noteworthy that she found no imitators, few admirers, and none who appeared to resent her inability to accept the prevailing social ideals. They were willing to wait for her to learn and to adjust.

Sex Problems

These may or may not be an apparent factor in the types of children we are calling 'maladjusted' in E.S.N. schools. Where they are not apparent, they may be hidden causes of much difficulty. The case notes will show that there are sex difficulties in some cases at least.

We are then, even in special schools, faced with the problem of children who cannot settle down; who are disturbing elements in their classes and potential dangers to other children; who are introverted; unready for social life; who are irritated and worn down by their contact with other people; and those who have built up an attitude of resentment and defiance. Without the help of a psychiatrist we must devise some means of helping them as far as our limited knowledge and skill can take us. Some have attempted to do this by using strict discipline, and certainly the very strict disciplinarian rarely seems to have one of these children in his class—or, rather, one of those with the more obvious behaviour difficulties. The schizoid type simply tends to withdraw more and more fully into himself when faced with a strong outside compelling authority. I have known of a developing case of schizophrenia in a girl of thirteen years (E.S.N.) which was treated with the utmost impatience and severity by a strong disciplinarian. The teacher's opinion was that the girl was trying to attract attention and simply needed compulsive discipline. Fortunately I was in the position to keep her with me most of the time and to insist upon sympathetic treatment, until she went into a mental hospital. By 'old-fashioned discipline' the disorders are suppressed, but not cured, and they emerge, whenever the outside control is removed, in far more acute forms. It is probable that sex disorders are often precipitated by the impact upon a maladjusted personality of a strong outside authority. If we wish to help in the building of a really stable character, even on a low intelligence level, we must let these personality disorders come into the open, and then try to find a means by which the child can himself deal with them. One of the most potent means is the establishment of a strong motive and desire for curing them.

Experiments with Free Play and Creative Activity

In our school we have been experimenting in the use of free play and creative activity in helping these maladjusted E.S.N. children to become stable personalities. In the beginning we had no idea that the I.Q. might appear to rise—our first thought was to help the class teacher by removing her difficult children, and to help the children by removing them from a more or less unsympathetic environment.

Our first experiment was with Ronald (I.Q. 45), who was a disturbing element in his class, and apparently very low grade, although he had already shown considerable ability in creative work. The experimental work is given in detail in the case notes, and it will be observed that the technique varied according to the needs and aptitudes of the individual. Some were given long periods in my room, some a day or two only. In the case of Rose, play-times only were used, including the midday break, i.e. one hour daily.

Treatment

The child was allowed to sit and do nothing until he wished to work or play. Then he was free to use paint with large brushes and as many large sheets of paper as he wanted, or modelling clay, plasticine, cardboard, puppets, percussion instruments (not available in the beginnings of the experiment) and occasionally I would put out bagatelle boards, etc. He was allowed to change his medium as often as he wished. Meanwhile I worked at my desk, always ready to answer questions, listen or discuss, but never addressing the child or taking the initiative. The child was not lonely, because of this readiness on my part, but he was allowed to go on in silence and solitude for as long as he wished. Gradually the soreness of friction with other people began to heal, and he himself began to seek companionship instead of having it forced upon him. In some cases, when this happened, he was ready to return to his class for a while. In other cases he needed a much longer period of freedom in work and play, as a rest from outside control. In the early stages I made no suggestions, but later he would begin to ask advice. I gave no orders,[1] and so resentment against authority gradually died down, until the child would begin spontaneously to ask permissions. E.S.N. children have comparatively few ideas and experiences to express, and although indiscreet interference and control has caused resentment and insecurity, and has, apparently, paralysed temporarily the child's capabilities, yet, after a time, freedom and self-imposed isolation begin to pall, and the child begins voluntarily to seek

[1] Modified in certain cases, and whenever children had to attend assemblies, etc.

stimuli from outside himself. By this time he has begun to have some faint realization of the value to himself of contact with other people, and he will begin, of his own volition, to find his way to social relationships. He will show signs when he is at this stage, and there is no need to hurry him. Social life is not to be forced upon him this time, but he himself is to seek it. It will perhaps be noticed that he begins to go out at play-time—or perhaps he only begins to talk more often to me and to explain his work, weaving stories round it. He may ask to go back to his class, or he may be happy for several children to come and work in our room. Occasionally there have been four or five maladjusted children working in my room at one time, each solitary if he pleases, but free to contact others when ready. I found clay modelling one of the most potent means of bringing them into contact. They would discuss, compare and to an extent, compete. I noticed that the tendency was to try to make the largest, strongest model—compensation, I suppose, for their own weakness and instability. Some of the clay work they did is shown in the accompanying photographs. When the experiment had been running for some time we introduced an occasional directed lesson, e.g. in painting, so that the children could get the 'flavour' of class work in a favourable atmosphere. Some of the painting was surprisingly original and thoughtful, and some showed an unexpected power of observation and expression. (The paintings, directed and perfectly free, are available for examination.) The children were not asked to attempt reading and number (occasionally they would ask for it, cf. Tony Green) as we were not so much giving remedial teaching in these subjects as trying to help the child to integrate his whole personality through free expression, play, and creative work; to use his latent capabilities; and finally to recognize his own need of other people so that he might be willing to co-operate with them as a useful and happy member of society. How far this was achieved in individual cases can be seen from the case notes.

From May 1950—very late in the experiment—we were fortunate in getting a visiting teacher of music and mime. She is an excellent pianist and musician, particularly interested in dramatic work and mime, and with experience of maladjusted children and spontaneous expression work in a war-time play centre, in junior clubs and in youth clubs. A 'maladjusted' mime group was formed, both of the children already in the experiment, and those on the waiting list for it. *The Sleeping Beauty* was mimed first, beautiful and expressive music being used. Because of the difficulty these children find in expressing themselves through speech, we used mime and movement to music, but we introduced a few words here and there. Gradually the children have become less shy and more able to use words and are now introducing quite an amount of speech spontaneously into their mimes. Even those with bad speech defects are using speech in the mime whenever they wish. No formal words are used, and the expression is still *chiefly* through movement, helped by the music. After six weeks of this work we were visited by a psychologist from overseas who particularly remarked upon the sincerity, co-operation and enjoyment shown by this group (the most difficult children in the school!) and upon the remarkable way they recognized their own musical cue and remembered their part. We are extending this work to include the whole school, on four afternoons weekly, with groups working in relays. The percussion work of the music group has also given the children a means of expression. (Note its effect upon Tony Green. See case notes.)

Of all the children who have taken part in this experiment, the most improvement has been shown by Ronald, for whom it was first started. He has learned to use his potentialities, and his I.Q. has thus appeared to rise from 42 at the age of seven to 89 at the age of twelve.

For three years his I.Q. appeared to be at imbecile level, and during the following eighteen months it rose to 89. At the age of ten years and eight months he did not know the names of the four primary colours, could do the educational nursery apparatus (e.g. fitting beakers, etc.) only with the utmost difficulty, could just about count objects up to ten, but recognized no symbols except 1, could not add 2 plus 1 mentally, could not recognize any coin but 1d. At the age of twelve he scored the following on the Burt Mental Arithmetic Tests:

Age	4–	5–	6–	7–
Score	10	10	10	—
	—	—	—	
	10	10	10	

He is now receiving attention from a child psychiatrist at a well-known hospital, and at the case conference the doctor gave the opinion that with further treatment his *apparent* I.Q. would probably rise another 20 points, provided he received no psychological setback.[1]

From our point of view, however, the whole success of Ronald's case is that a social misfit and potential homosexual, now takes his place as a happily co-operating member of his class.

In other cases there has been a rise in the I.Q., though a less spectacular one, and also an advance in academic attainment, although we have not attempted to teach ordinary school subjects. But in each case, without exception there has been a gradual blossoming of the personality, a more joyful and co-operative attitude, a greater confidence, and a movement towards social contact, which are the very qualities we set out to foster.

Details of the methods used in individual cases, and the response of the child to the experiment are given in the following case notes.

[1] Details of Ronald's development are given below in a full case study.

RONALD

Detailed notes made by the head teacher during the experimental work done with Ronald.

Chronological age	Mental age	I.Q.	
7 years	2 yrs. 9 mths.	42	At these ages the child
8 ,,	3 ,, 8 ,,	45	should have been reported
9 ,,	4 ,, 2 ,,	45	as ineducable.
10 ,,	5 ,, 6 ,,	55	
10 yrs. 8 mths.	5 ,, 10 ,,	54	

EXPERIMENT BEGINS

| 11 yrs. 3 mths. | 7 yrs. 6 mths. | 67 |
| 12 ,, 4 ,, | 11 ,, – ,, | 89 |

At this point Ronald was 'deascertained' and returned to a secondary modern school, where he fits in quite well.

Development. Age of speaking—2 years.

Age of walking—1 year 3 months.

Parents. Both intelligent, interested and co-operative.

General Behaviour. November 1948. Mental Age—5 years 10 months.

Ronald is of low I.Q. (54—recently risen from 45) and has been very unfavourably reported upon by his class teacher. He is very lazy—no application nor concentration except in art subjects. Extremely babyish and easily upset by other children —yet in some ways very pugnacious. Seems very feminine also.

Seems to have an extreme friendship with another boy. Says Robert forces him to play with him, etc. Query—*is* he forced, or does he attract Robert purposely and sun himself in his obvious admiration? No doubt he is now rather afraid of Robert, who is stronger and a bully, but no doubt that he also depends upon Robert to protect him, to follow his lead and to bolster him up. This tendency to accept the admiration and attentions of another boy gives some anxiety as to his future. Robert will stroke his face or kiss him if he thinks he is unobserved.

Ronald seems precocious in many ways. For one of his very

low intelligence he is exceptionally well-informed, observant and original. He is especially precocious in matters of sex. This, with his obvious attraction for other boys and his femininity, constitutes a great danger for himself and other boys, unless it can be very wisely and carefully controlled and directed. Unfortunately Ronald is almost incapable of working under direction, and it will be more difficult to influence him than is usual with children.

In class, Ronald is the master of an undercurrent. He is *incapable*, at present, of submitting to the routine and discipline of community life. So, in class he is largely at a loss, in spite of the individual methods used here. His teacher (who is not yet experienced) finds an 'atmosphere' pervading the class according to Ronald's mood. He is too timid to rebel openly, but continually asks, 'Why do us poor boys have to go to school?' and manages to convey to the other children his own sense of being hard-done-by. He causes sniggers to run round the class when, for example, a picture of a little girl undressing is in his reading book. The other boys follow him about, probably hoping for information which Ronald can give them. (Ronald drew in his rough work book several 'rude' pictures, which showed an amazing familiarity with the female nude figure, and a quite astonishing degree of sophistication, e.g. A nude man and woman 'jitterbugging'. His productions are far from the usual 'rude drawing' of the ordinary school boy.

His teacher has asked for his removal, on the grounds that he is teaching the others to snigger and laugh about sex matters, even in their most everyday forms.

Work. Art and constructional work *excellent*.

Other Subjects. Has shown no interest or ability in any other subject but art.

Test made in October 1948. Age 10 years 8 months. The educational apparatus used in the nursery class he does *very* slowly. Mosaic square took him the whole morning.

Does not know the names of four primary colours though his practical colour work is excellent.

Number. Can count objects up to ten (this is an advance). No symbols except 1.

Cannot add 2 plus 1 mentally.

Does not recognize any coins except 1*d*.

Cannot write name.

February 1949. Can now recognize and put objects corresponding to symbols 1–10.

Can give mentally 2 plus 1, 2 plus 3, 2 minus 1, etc.

Recognizes ½*d*.

Sounds—a, e, i, o, u, only.

Query. Now he is eleven, should he go to occupation centre or to boys' school?

For occupation centre (1) Very low I.Q.
(2) Practically no progress in 'school' subjects during three years.
(3) Inability to take his place in class and among other boys.

For school (1) *Slight* progress in last few weeks.
(2) Exceptional art and handwork ability, though these can only be done if he is left *entirely* free. Cannot measure, etc.

Suggestion. He should remain here for a while longer, and be given every opportunity to develop his special talents, even to the exclusion of other subjects.

Experiment

Ronald removed from class, and put in my room, with choice of paper, paint, cardboard and clay. To develop *freely* on his own lines.

It has become obvious that Ronald cannot do his creative work while being expected to do even a minimum of number, etc., nor under direction. Given the chance to create freely, how will his talent develop?

Painting. Ronald produces an enormous quantity of work, much of it highly imaginative and of a high order for a child. He has a reputation for laziness—instead he is working steadily all day till about 2.30 p.m. when he clears up and sits down, saying he is 'worn out'. He may well be worn out, seeing the speed and originality of his work.

'The Lost World'—imaginative reproduction of story heard on wireless. Colour, design and narrative excellently expressed.

'Fields'—dark frowning and strange colour. 'Hawaii'—scene among palms on sea-shore. 'Clown'—'Fair'—also many scenes in which strange new animals are shown. Ronald can give the names and special characteristics of his 'new' animals. They show great originality and inventiveness. 'Heaven' shows us 'where the dead fishes go.'

Gradually the quality falls off. It seems as if his need has worked itself out. There is still originality but his interest is now spent, and he has not the patience to transmit his ideas through paint.

Cardboard. The old Punch and Judy show is shown to him as being in need of renovation. With a new burst of energy he works all day remaking it. He designed and made a Punch and Judy of cardboard and bunting, and amuses himself by giving a show with them.

Having seen my store of cardboard, he is inspired afresh, and spends days building houses—a school, an hotel, two bungalows and a block of offices. He cannot measure, but cuts very accurately. Some houses have two floors, each furnished with cardboard furniture. The houses are of very original design, with, usually, flat roofs for roof gardens, and projecting to give shade in summer. A road is made with street lamps—but the quality here is poor. The school has a playground with swings, giant strides, a sand pit, etc. This

MISFITS IN THE SPECIAL E.S.N. SCHOOL

I think, is an indication of what a child asks for in a playground. Production of houses is only limited by the space we have for keeping them!

I suggest he should use up some spare pieces which are wasting, and he makes jointed puppets with strings. No great success in working them.

When Ronald is not deeply absorbed I send him on messages, etc.—and he begins to be more reliable and sensible.

He is allowed to stay in or go to play as he wishes, but he is entirely separated from Robert.

Ronald now begins to flag where creative work is concerned. He asks only to play bagatelle. I give him a box of cut-out figures and counters, and ask him to arrange the figures and put the counters by them. He seems quite pleased to do so. Then I show him how to build a sum with figures and counters, e.g. 2 plus 1 equals 3 and to copy it on paper. Soon he is able to do a page of such sums—*making them up for himself*. He will now spend his day doing this quite gladly. Learns to subtract in same simple manner. *Note.*— Probably art would be of a higher quality than arithmetic. I am perfectly ready for him to discard academic subjects entirely for art subjects *but*—

(1) he begins to flag at art. His mental capacity apparently will not feed his talent for long enough for him to do work of his own invention continually. He needs help from outside himself, but this is just what he is, so far, incapable of accepting and using.

(2) For the first time he is *willingly* accepting direction (e.g. the suggestion that he should learn how to build up 'sums') and is turning this outside direction to his own power of invention. This may be very useful to him in *developing* his art talent. His willingness to co-operate rather than to be his own complete law, must be encouraged.

(3) If his ability in handwork is to develop, he will need a knowledge of number for use in measuring, etc.

88   EDUCATING THE SUB-NORMAL CHILD

Summer Term. Ronald says he has 'gone off painting' and wants to do sums. Says he has found out how to tell the time (to a great extent he has) and what the prices in the shop mean. Typically Ronald—'Nobody taught me, it just came to me'!

Ronald spends day doing 'sums'. Seems to have no other ambition at the moment. Obviously this phase *can be used* but is, in itself, likely to prove a dead end for him, since his mathematical capacity is practically nil.

Obviously he is now in the mood for aquiring skills from outside.

Experimentally—Ronald is put into class again (*not* the same class).

3.4.49. (*a*) Can he now 'fit in'?
(*b*) Is he willing to be taught and to work under direction?
(*c*) Will his artistic work suffer, or will he be able to feed his creative talent with what he acquires from class work?

12.4.49. Ronald appears to fit in. Works very well—is willing even to be 'told'.

Great difficulty with coins, but tries very hard.

Asked to find out something about wool. Next day Ronald tells story of sheep farm—sheep shearing—knows correct terms, and story is coherent and accurate. Asked where he found it out—from books? No—cannot read. Who told you about it? Nobody—I just knew (typically Ronald who cannot learn from outside himself). Teacher explains carefully how *she* has to learn from books, etc. Ronald admits then that he has seen sheep farm on pictures, and has learned about it that way. *N.B.—Admits* outside influence.

Tries out his usual method of causing giggling, etc., in class. A little girl has a doll under her desk. Its legs protrude from desk. Ronald comes to teacher and says Kathleen has a rude thing under her desk. Teacher appears puzzled—what sort of thing? Ronald—A doll with no clothes on. Teacher says

MISFITS IN THE SPECIAL E.S.N. SCHOOL

bring it here—looks at it—cannot see what is rude about it. Ronald seems a bit crestfallen. Reiterates it has no clothes—it's a rude thing. Teacher still appears puzzled—it's only a doll—nothing rude about it—appeals to class. Class agree it is not rude—Ronald returns to place very flattened. For perhaps the first time he has failed to raise a laugh at his 'rude' remarks.

Note.—This line would have been impossible to take in his old class where he had many followers. The giggle or burst of furtive laughter would come before the teacher had a chance to deal with it.

Art work. Ronald settled down with clay-modelling group and produces a snake. Head well observed and well formed—whole lacks nothing of his usual virility, and yet seems to have gained something in technique.

18.4.49. Ronald can barely manage the 'sums' he was formerly making for himself. Seems utterly at a loss now in number work. Obviously this phase has played itself out.

Decide to put him back on 'free work' in my room, except for P.T. and such narrative lessons as will feed his creative ability.

23.5.49. Ronald returns to solitude and creative work, but *very reluctantly*—I find that his mother has impressed upon him that painting, etc., are no good. *Sums* are what will get him on. This is probably the partial cause of his sustained efforts to do number. He imagines that he is to go to a boys' school after the summer holiday, and that in such a school he will get the cane if he gets his sums wrong! Some time is devoted to explaining that this idea is quite mistaken.

More time in explaining different kinds of cleverness, e.g. Beethoven who could not do sums even when old. Reproductions of work of famous artists shown. Ronald seems reassured.

Given a choice of materials he decides to build an

aeroplane in cardboard. Works in absolute absorption for a whole day. Technique shows marked improvement.

Is left alone with another boy for most of day, and hardly a word passes between them. Both are completely absorbed in their work. (The other boy is making clay models.)

24.5.49. Aeroplane finished—span of wings 4 ft. Length of body 4 ft. 6 in. Seats inside—doors with handles which turn (made of paper fasteners). Engines and propellers on wings —exhaust pipe (?) in nose of plane. Finished by 11.30 a.m. Very roughly made, of course, but remarkable for his age and I.Q. Starts immediately upon clay work. Produces a 'boxer'.

29.5.49. Asks for cardboard and makes an engine. Rather old-fashioned engine shape. Puts an 'arm' on side (it should work the wheels but there is no connexion. In *itself* it works quite well.) New wheel technique, makes a cross for spokes, and puts outside ring, joining it rather cleverly to the spokes.

With waste cardboard makes a man sawing a tree. He moves and his saw goes backwards and forwards.

2.6.49. Sees the new clay and decides to use it. No good work produced by the end of the morning.

3.6.49. Asks for cardboard to make a car. Long thought about wheels—those on his engine won't go round so a new type must be thought out. While working on car, he informs me that our school is not very 'posh'. It ought to be like a palace and then the boys would have good manners, and be good. He thinks he is already good, but others would be better if the school was 'posh'. Playground should have swings, etc., because 'we haven't anything to play with, madam'. I ask him if one day he will make a model of the school he would like.

Soon after, he says, 'This is a very complicated car. Would you mind if I left it?' He promises to finish it later, but his mind is obviously on model school, so I give permission.

MISFITS IN THE SPECIAL E.S.N. SCHOOL

Model school has a swimming-pool and diving-board, and a small boy has 'sneaked out of school' to swim! Note here—Ronald's fear of ghosts comes to the fore. He makes a boy watching to see if any ghosts are coming. Opportunity to explain matters to him.

Ronald and Fred Brown now speak more, but in explaining their models and exchanging ideas. No fooling goes on even when they are left. Both find their work absorbing.

Ronald has large sheet of card as basis for his model.

Fred has small sheet for castle.

Ronald tells me that his sheet is his country, and Fred's sheet is *his* world. 'My country is bigger than Fred's.' Ronald is not too pleased that Fred is able to make models as well as he can. Does not like anybody else to attract attention.

Whitsun Holiday

June 13th to 24th. Ronald produces a 'ballet'. Theatre and figures on strings to dance.

Visit to Zoo—Ronald's reactions are disappointing. Takes comparatively little interest, though very excited.

After the Zoo—Fred makes animals in clay. Ronald says Fred should make lion roaring as we saw him. I suggest Ronald makes it. Excellent roaring lion produced.

Then Ronald makes large castle complete with guns and soldiers. Works hours making horse and foot soldiers. Very anxious that his castle should be preferred to Fred's! Shows very great concentration and works extremely hard.

30.6.49. Suggest vases should be made.

1.7.49 to 14.7.49. Ronald does coiled and finger-built pottery. Good work, but does not—or cannot—brook any suggestion. Soon tires of pottery and asks for cardboard. Builds a bridge.

Then back to painting. (A little pub where I and my mother and auntie went.)

N.B.—Ronald paid dinner money in next room. Later 2*d.* change was sent in for him. I said, Ronald pays 5*d.* for dinner, so should only have 1*d.* change. Immediately Ronald said—Yes, but I brought 1*s.* 0*d.* (i.e. for two days). Ordinarily Ronald knows nothing at all about money, nor can he add nor subtract. Is this really a defect, or is it due to some deep-seated psychological cause?

September to October 1949. Ronald prefers to work in classroom. Wants to learn to knit.

Note.—Ronald wants to learn! It has not 'just come to him'. This should be the first step to a more normal attitude.

Ronald will do nothing but knit—says he can only learn one thing at a time. I believe he is right there.

October. Ronald involved in a gang. On the whole he is afraid to fight, but is always to be found in the company of the school 'strong man'. The strong men seem to vie for Ronald's favour. He has been seen directing them to attack (in a gang), but is always discreetly hidden behind a coping when the trouble starts.

October 1949. Ronald's father (just home from abroad) visits school to tell us what a very great improvement he has noticed in him. We have noted academic improvements, but still more his change of attitude.

He is now willing to admit his need to learn from outside himself, which in my opinion was his most pressing need. I believe that his handicap consisted in this attitude, together with such a desire to excel that he was *incapable* of attempting anything at which he might fail. Therefore he was able to attempt and carry out imaginative art work and constructional work which he knew he could do better than the other boys and without any advice or help, but was *unable* (not just 'unwilling') to attempt reading and number work for which he had to rely upon outside instruction, and in which he knew other boys could surpass him.

Ronald   Fred Brown

Ronald   Fred Brown

| Fred Brown | Teddie | John | Ronald | Tony |

| Ronald | Michael | Alan | Jimmie |

Free expression work in clay. Mal-adjusted group

MISFITS IN THE SPECIAL E.S.N. SCHOOL 93

It seems probable that psychological treatment could deal with this attitude of mind (which already is less marked than formerly) and that he might possibly prove to be normal in intelligence if this handicap could be dealt with.

October 29th to November 6th. At Camp.

November 14th. Returns to school. Says he did not like camp and is very glad to be back. Appears heavy and stupid. Impossible to rouse him. Away ill.

21.11.49 Ronald returns to school. Still heavy, dull and apathetic. Looks pale and shows no interest or spark of life.

22.11.49. Returns to individual free expression in my room. Is very glad to paint. Produces much—weight lifter, Father Christmas, Christmas tree with children, etc.

In classroom for half afternoon. Teacher reports that he is more lively and interested—joins in dramatic work.

22.11.49 to 25.11.49. Continues with painting—returns to class for midday meal and whenever it is necessary for me to clear my room for interviews, etc. Teacher reports that Ronald is back to his former liveliness. Is interested and ready to talk. Entertains class in dramatic work, etc.

24.11.49. Ronald produces green elephant. Other children question colour, but he persists. The shape, stance and character are excellent. He also produces Nativity picture (stimulus—previous afternoon's practice for Nativity play and suggestion from me that such a picture would be interesting). Colouring and design of clouds, hills, etc., most unusual and interesting.

Prefers to paint rather than to take part in group of clay modellers.

25.11.49. Chooses clay modelling. Produces 'Angel Gabriel'. Begins to try to shape legs and body—says he does not want to make them straight and asks for modelling tool. Torso of Angel is modelled with some knowledge of human form. He says he is putting a skirt on it, as it is a man angel, and they did not wear trousers then.

28.11.49 to 30.11.49. More modelling. Colossal figure of a man who is so strong he can lift a horse. Ronald refuses to believe that this strong man will break up because he has made it in parts and joined them. Hands and fingers are attempted. (Actually man cracked and fell during drying, but Ronald only laughed. He seemed to take a certain pleasure in the downfall of the strong. I note that the weaker the boy, the more he tries to make massive models.)

30.11.49. Ronald decides to model the stable in clay. Put supporting pillars at corners, but finds roof caves in (used to building in cardboard—has not understood different medium). It is pointed out that more strengthening pillars are needed. Ronald says, 'I am doing it *this* way.' Roof still collapses and he consigns it to the clay bin. His inability to accept advice still handicaps him.

Meanwhile—he returns to class occasionally and answers among the few best in mental arithmetic. He is beginning to be able to do creative work alongside classwork—a great advance.

In discussion Ronald is the only child who can give the *most important* difference between a bird and an aeroplane, i.e. that a bird has life in it.

30.11.49. A series of large animal paintings. Noah's ark. Slapdash work. This is pointed out to him, and he begins again, working carefully and yet showing as much enthusiasm and 'inspiration' as before.

Obviously his work *need* not be slapdash, and his originality loses nothing if his work is careful.

From this time Ronald's work is careful and painstaking. His colour work shows definite improvement, and he begins to maintain his high standard of creative work while working also as a lively and active member of his class.

He can now brook constructive criticism, and will, very occasionally, ask advice.

MISFITS IN THE SPECIAL E.S.N. SCHOOL

Tests.	May 1949	December 1949
Parrot counting to	12	100
Symbols recognized to	nil	100 (a few mistakes)
Burt Mental Arithmetic Tests		
Age 4–	7/10	10/10
Age 5–	7/10	8/10
Age 6–	2/10	7/10
Age 7–	nil	nil
Written Arithmetic	nil	Units, addition and Subtraction
Coin Recognition	—	—

January to April 1950. Ronald now takes his place as an ordinary member of his class. He neither seeks nor appreciates special treatment. His art work has not suffered, but while living a normal class life, and while taking an interest in ordinary class work, he is producing original, richly coloured and careful art work.

His conversation is unusually intelligent for these E.S.N. children, and he is extremely well-informed.

Ronald still chooses a strong 'he-man' for his close friend, but the fact that he is older than the other children has encouraged him to stand on his own feet more. He is not quite so girlish as he was.

April 1950. Ronald is taking a keen interest in our guinea pigs and other pets. I notice that he can discuss his hope that they will breed without any of his former sniggering.

Ronald is dinner monitor and shows much sense and initiative in this job.

May 1950. Ronald is chief 'keeper' of the pets. He shows a good sense of responsibility, and each day teaches a new boy how to clean out cages, and how to feed them, etc.

Works desperately at arithmetic. Excellent (E.S.N. standard!) at mental arithmetic, e.g. gives instantly correct answer to $1s. 0d. - 8\frac{1}{2}d. =$ but cannot *write* sums, unless teacher is watching him. Can work them on blackboard, paper, or book without help or suggestion, if only teacher stands by. If left entirely alone he writes absolute rubbish, even though desperately anxious to succeed.

Emotional difficulty rather than intellectual?

May 11th. Teacher reports that he is beginning to know words in reading. Has previously shown no reading ability at all. Great step forward. His mental arithmetic is one of the best in the class.

Language remains unusual for sub-normal, e.g. speaks of making a 'complicated' engine for a ship. Speaks correctly of 'constructing' a boat and 'the structure' of a ship.

Said: 'Rabbits don't need water. They get enough *moisture* from the green leaves.'

Brought two fishes to school, 'I was going to bring one, but I thought it would be so desperately lonely.'

June 14th. Examined for special defect by school doctor.
Mental Age 11   Chronological Age $12\frac{4}{12}$ I.Q. 89.

June 20th. Came up to me and said, 'Madam, I want to give you some advice.' Gave advice as to the training of the guinea pigs in using their staircase.

June 22nd. Constructing 'a fair'—bumping cars, etc., from cardboard. Ready and willing to return to classwork.

Tests: Burt Mental Arithmetic	Age	4–	5–	6–	7–
	Score	10	10	10	
		—	—	—	nil
		10	10	10	

Burt Reading Tests	Age	4–	4–	6–	7–
	Score	—	—	—	—

Knows only nine letters.

July 1950. Expects to be transferred to ordinary secondary school after summer holiday. Draws picture of head teacher at her desk in 'experiment' room as parting gift. 'When I'm not here and she wonders how I'm getting on, she'll be able to look at it and remember me.'

September 1950. 'Deascertainment' held up so Ronald returns. Appointment made for psychological treatment at hospital. Case conference held (head teacher present)—much interest shown in unusual case. Ronald recommended for normal secondary modern school.[1]

Meanwhile, while painting a moonlit scene he informed me that the moon has no light really. It shines with the reflected light of the sun, which is on the other side of the world.

Ronald shows much talent for mime. Chooses part of 'Mirror on the Wall' in 'Snow White'. Imitates action of queen sewing, without moving from his place by wall—obviously expresses as well as he can the spirit and function of a mirror. His dramatic work is excellent.

CASE STUDY

Detailed study of the effect of the experimental treatment upon the special difficulties of Fred Brown.

FRED BROWN

Mental Age, 6 years 6 months. Chronological Age, 9 years. I.Q. 72.

Development.

Speech—no record.

Walking—1 year.

Clean and dry—18 months.

---

[1] September 1952. Ronald has been at an ordinary secondary school for more than a year, and I understand that he is doing well there.

Mother. Rather poor intelligence, heavy mind and, I would say, lacking in sympathetic understanding. Yet well-meaning and tries to do her best for children. Overburdened—Fred and five younger children and another expected. Takes the trouble to bring Fred to school, as he persistently and purposely misses the guide. Finds the daily journey burdensome, as she has to take the other children to school first, and to get her mother-in-law to mind the younger ones. Says she gets the children up in time, but they 'keep whining', and will not hurry.

Father. According to mother he takes no interest in the children, and gives her no help. Sometimes asks why she worries over such a little thing, when Fred truants, or comes home at 11 p.m. At other times he will arouse himself from his lethargy and beat Fred. It has no effect. The Special Officer has tried to contact father but has never found him in.

Home Situation. Mother says her mother-in-law is the greatest difficulty. She insists on interfering between mother and children, and makes trouble between husband and wife. I should imagine the home atmosphere is one of contention, discord and 'whining'. It is hardly surprising that Fred 'bunks out', and remains out till bedtime.

Truancy. As Fred is developing the habit of truancy I asked that a special guide should be provided to escort him from door to door. This was refused, and the boy was brought by his mother when she could get hold of him. Often he gave her the slip and spent the day with truanters from ordinary schools. This is how he was led into breaking into a shop and stealing. In view of the home situation and the mother's inability to cope, together with her approaching confinement, Fred was recommended for a residential E.S.N. school.

Fred.

Past history: 1. Always late. No reward or punishment will help him to come early. Is sent out early to meet guide at bus

MISFITS IN THE SPECIAL E.S.N. SCHOOL

stop, since she is not allowed to call for him at his house, but misses her—mother has to bring him often half-way through morning. Given responsible job to do first thing—still fails to arrive. Will not allow anything to please or to hurt himself—seems to retire within and just gives a secret smile whether he is praised or blamed.

2. Lateness now becomes truancy. Runs off and does not return home in time for school. Is this objection to being 'guided'? Try letting him travel alone. Works for a few days —then truancy. Actually hides from mother. Mother phones each day to ask if he has come.

3. Evenings—he runs out and 'bunks' into pictures. Does not return till cinema shuts. In company of other likeminded boys.

Returns home with one shilling—says a man has given it to him. Father *intends* to investigate matter—nothing done however.

4. Invents long story when I inquire into these things. Will not admit to liking his mother—dislikes whole family except baby, and would be glad to go into a 'home'.

5. In new class—works quietly and well, but is brought daily by his mother—not till after 10 a.m. as she has four younger children.

6. After long habit has been formed (of regular though late attendance) I suggest that he should try coming alone again—like the other boys. Mother reluctantly agrees— *the first day, he truants.*

Note.—Has Fred lived too crowded a life for one of his temperament? Never alone at home, at school, on way to school. Does he need solitude to heal the friction caused by relationships with other people, and to develop his creative powers?

19.5.49. Starts 'living' in my room. At first he is allowed to sit quietly doing nothing. After a time he is offered paint, clay, etc. Chooses clay (he has already shown talent in art, especially clay work). Immediately sets to work with absorbed interest. Produces in one and a half days an elephant carrying two boys, a baby elephant ridden by a younger boy, a bull, a lion, a snake coiled round a tree, a parrot, a monkey with a basket, and a rock with small caves in which tiny squirrels live. All this work is 'alive', though his technique fails in portraying parrot and monkey. Decides to paint these, allowing the week-end for drying.

23.5.49. Begins to paint models. His colouring is vivid and attractive, though he has the custom of colouring parts of animals in various colours, e.g. bull—red body—yellow head —green horns.

Fred is perfectly happy in this creative work. He can be left in the room alone, or with another boy, and will continue to work without slackening for a whole day. Hums and talks softly to himself while working.

24.5.49. Fred begins to talk freely while working—conversation always about the work he is doing. Begins to be very helpful also. Makes it his business to see rubber mats are spread, so that clay will not get on floor, etc. Does this for others who are working in here also. Offers to get water pots, etc., for others. Social attitude is changing.

25.5.49. Fred brings cigarette cards and 'comics' to illustrate things he has told us about during his work.

27.5.49. Clay runs out. Fred has to paint. Makes no move towards cardboard modelling, although Ronald is creating trains, etc., in this medium.

30.5.49. Fred is still perfectly happy in here. Has as yet no wish to return to community life and 'work' in the usual sense of the word.

Test. Before Fred was brought in here, I tested him on Burt's Mental Arithmetic Tests. His score was:

Year 4–	10 right.
Year 5–	10 right
Year 6–	7 right but taking a long time to work them out.

Ronald   Tony   Teddie   Teddie

Michael   Tony   Ronald   Fred Brown

Jimmie—first experiment with clay

Free expression work in clay. Mal-adjusted group

MISFITS IN THE SPECIAL E.S.N. SCHOOL

31.5.49. Year 6– 9 right immediately. (Failed to write 35. Wrote 53 instead.) Tested on the Binet Stanford Tests (London Revision) he scores as follows:
Mental Age 6 years 8 months. Chronological Age 9 years. I.Q. 73.

Earlier Tests

28.9.48. 5 years 10 months. 8 years 4 months. I.Q. 70.
16.3.48. 5 years 10 months. 7 years 10 months. I.Q. 74.

1.6.49. Fred's personality is blossoming. Instead of being shut up within himself, he is getting friendly—shares a joke—smiles and laughs and comes forward with his tale quite readily.

Clay arrives—great excitement from Fred. He carries it in, breaks it up, damps it, etc. Actually calls to me across the hall! Full of fun and high spirits. Almost unrecognizable with his bright eyes and colour.

2.6.49. Brought a book to school yesterday (his birthday present.) Picture of a Crusader in it. 'Copies' it in clay. Today 'copies' Crusader on horse. Really is spirit in the way he holds his sword high above his head.

Fred stands looking at his work, and singing at the top of his voice. (I have never heard more than a hum before. His singing this morning is really rather beautiful.) He is full of the exultation of a work satisfactorily achieved. He is, however, perfectly happy to allow me to run a wire through the sword and arm to prevent its breaking, and welcomes the suggestion that a *larger* shield would rest on the horse's back, and so strengthen the shield arm.

Immediately begins new model while Crusader hardens. Makes boy at Zoo—has bun in his hand—pelican comes and takes bun while he is not looking. Fred has real sense of humour, but with a certain malice in it. Says the boy has only the fare home and cannot get another bun or any other food.

3.6.49. Fred arrives looking glum. Does not ask for clay. On being asked what work he wants, he inquires whether there is any plasticine. I give him various colours.

He makes a castle—gate guarded by a dragon. A light goes on over the gate whenever anybody approaches. A guard on horseback watches the dragon. Guard falls asleep. Dragon goes to gate. He thinks he can get out. (I reply—'But he can't'—thinking this is the expected reply.) Fred says, 'Yes he can—he's found the key.' He makes a key and puts it on the dragon's back so that he can escape. Later Fred opens the gate and says, 'Somebody has opened the gate, but the dragon had fallen asleep and did not know it was open.'

4.6.49 to 30.6.49. Production slows up—then goes forward in jerks. I consider wisdom of sending him back to class for mornings only. Then he spurts again.

Visit to Zoo. On return Fred makes clay and plasticine animals. Spirited and easily recognizable attempts.

Makes a castle *à la* Ronald.

30.6.49. Suggest making pottery. Immediately uses incised decoration.

1.7.49 to 14.7.49. Shows talent in making coiled and finger-built vases. Begins to appear rather at loose end.

14.7.49. Given a page of 'sums'—all correct (addition and subtraction). I ask him to draw boy and elephant. Then to make a story about it. He gives two good sentences which I print, and he reads them back to me before copying them. I point out to him that he can now read. We make up a sum about the boys' spendings at the Zoo, one shilling to spend. He is rather slow about money, but the story form seems to attract him. (He has always built an elaborate story round his models.) Experiment with a story project each day, building reading and number on it. Fred no longer dislikes school, and, although he cannot resist the temptation to wander off on his own pursuits, his truancy is less frequent. We hope,

MISFITS IN THE SPECIAL E.S.N. SCHOOL

in time, that he will outgrow the habit—but the time has not come yet. We must give him longer.

Summer Holiday.

29.8.49. School reopens.

8.9.49. Fred committed to the care of L.E.A. for out-of-school delinquency.

Note.—His delinquency is the direct result of truancy. He met other truants and was led into house-breaking.

If he had been allowed a special guide, he would never have developed these habits of truancy and consequent delinquency. How necessary it is to spend public money in prevention rather than to wait for actual delinquency.

TONY GREEN

Date of Test	Chronological Age	Mental Age	I.Q.
19.10.49	8 years	6 years	75
6. 9.50	8 years 11 months	8 years 2 months	92

General character. Absent and withdrawn. Simply does not hear when spoken to and is obviously engrossed in some world of his own. Does not appear to care for approval or reproof. Solitary in habits—seems hardly to recognize the existence of other people. Yet when he *does* wake up, he is rough, noisy and ill-mannered (e.g. spits, does not use his handkerchief, etc. No foundation for these habits, apparently, in home background. Also pushes other children, etc. No real aggressiveness—just a very rough noisy outlet when he emerges from his own world at all.)

In Class. If he will join in at all, he talks most intelligently, e.g. gives very interesting answers when we have discussions and conversations. Is obviously very intelligent (i.e. on Special School standards), but his withdrawal and absent-mindedness make him very tiresome and difficult to cope with in a class. He loves stories, and his only attempts at social contacts are made in trying to get a younger and very dull boy to act the plays he creates. Hates music and movement lessons and usually has to be removed.

June 8th, 1950. Taken to H.T.'s room for special treatment. Given a choice of materials, drawing, clay, painting, etc.—no result. Shows little interest.

June 9th. Michael[1] is also in room. Shows an interest in Tony, but no response. I suggest Tony might like to teach Michael to act plays—very poor response. Not willing to tell stories to Michael either.

June 12th. Shows interest in books. Takes books freely from my bookshelf and looks at them. Acquires a heap of books which he hoards in his box.

June 13th. Given puppets—no result. Chief object is to 'mess about' and go from one thing to another without interest or concentration.

June 13th. Finds books of history pictures. Immediate interest and response. Comes to show them to me, and talks of history, pirates, etc. Full of excitement and seems ready for creative work. Suggest that he should make a story about pirates. Give him sheets of paper and we staple them into a book. Says he cannot draw a pirate (he obviously would be too critical of his own attempt to enjoy making it) so I let him trace a picture. Concentrated work for the first time. He gives me original and realistic sentences, which I write for him to copy into his book. He copies very carefully, and shows much pride in his work.

June 14th. Tony prefers to 'read' rather than to do another page of his book. Obviously needs reading, and is interested in learning to read. Meanwhile his ability must be fed through stories. He longs for stories, lives through them. Begs also for 'history'. I take the history picture books, and

[1] Michael is a younger child, anti-social and destructive who is taking part in this experimental treatment.

tell him the stories attached to each picture. Appears willing to listen for as long as I can tell them. Rather disturbed by Michael, who has no interest in history, and follows his own noisy pursuits.

June 15th and 16th. I have a class in my room. Tony continually tells me that he will be glad when I have no class. Obviously enjoys solitude.

June 19th to 23rd. Tony begins to link up with Michael, playing on the rocking-horse with drum and other instruments. Now seems to have no wish but to join in Michael's baby play. Occasionally will paint, 'read', ask for stories and history—but prefers to be rather noisy and riotous with Michael. The two co-operate in a few battle scenes and pirate stories, but mostly they take drums and ride the horse.

June 27th. Interests remain rather scattered, but is beginning to tire of Michael and his distracting toys and play. Brings pictures of pirates to me to talk them over. Is very interested. Gets impatient with Michael's interruptions. Tony obviously needs quiet, and one person's full attention.

June 29th. Traces a pirate ship. Asked what sentence he wants to write under it, he suddenly embarks upon a full, and very imaginative story of pirates, acting it as he goes, using a sinister voice when necessary, and entering thoroughly into the spirit of the thing. Ends up, 'So now you know what a pirate's like!'

Quite obviously Tony finds speech the easiest medium of expression, and needs as much freedom and opportunity as possible. He is less withdrawn, and comes completely out of his shell in telling this story. Is in a high state of excitement during the story—face very red and words become almost unintelligible—yet changes of voice and demeanour continue. Speech and dramatic work is obviously his medium.

June 30th. Tony is less anxious to join in Michael's baby play today. Seems to be settling to more serious work.

Voluntarily tidies his own shelf. Settles down to 'reading' a large pile of books.

July 3rd. Continues 'reading'. Does some work on his pirate book. Michael is occupied, so Tony can, and does, concentrate through the day. I ask him whether he would like to join the mime class—which he often watches from my door. He refuses. Says he likes to act his own stories by himself, but not plays with the others.

July 4th. 'Reads' Eagle Comic to me, i.e. reads easy words while I supply longer words. Begins to build up unknown words. Asks for more history, and spends much time listening to history stories (has good memory for these stories).

Says his mother will help him to read. Likes his mother, but not father, 'because he hits you'. He says father does not help him to read—says with rather scornful enjoyment, 'He can't read himself.' Father does not only hit him when he is naughty, but 'by accident' at other times. This is the first information Tony has volunteered about his home life.

July 6th. Tony continues to ask for 'history'. Still resents my having a class during the absence of a teacher. Obviously needs the care and attention and interest of one person.

Begins to take an interest in the percussion band. Tony has always 'slept' during music lesson (and during the reign of a former teacher of music and movement he behaved so badly that I had to remove him). So I have not, so far, asked him to go to music lessons. Sometimes I have asked him whether he wants to go, but the reply is always emphatically no. He will bang a drum while riding the rocking-horse, but never would consent to do so during the music lesson. One class is playing 'Gnomes Dance' from *Peer Gynt* on the percussion band. Tony always wakes up, and sometimes moves about my room in response to the rhythm when this is being played. Today he said, 'I love this' when it began. I advised him to stand outside my door and listen to it, which he did with obvious enjoyment, making small movements to express the rhythm.

July 6th to end of term. Part of this time I have a class, which Tony dislikes intensely. He continues to go to the door when he hears the 'Gnomes Dance'. At last he says, 'I ought to go out to this.' I send him out, and he joins in with high colour and bright eyes, obviously enjoying every moment of it. He co-operates well, and, at last, is fully 'awake' in a social co-operative effort. This may be the beginning of great things for him.

Shows great interest still in reading. Comes to me to read a short easy story as often as he wishes. Tires, and fails at recognizing words, rather soon, but his interest does not flag. Can build easy words, but seems to have, so far, no memory for whole word units. I am interested to know how he can have failed to learn to read in his ordinary school, as he is so keen. He says the teacher at the other school always gave him copying to do instead of teaching him to read. It is evident that he has the ability to learn to read, but his interests are no longer centred in home—mother—baby, etc., which are the interest centres of the usual introductory reader. Needs books just as easy, but based on pirates, Red Indians, etc.

Tony has always refused to take part in mime (maladjusted group). Suddenly decides to join the class, and does so whole-heartedly. This is his second step towards co-operating with his fellows.

September 1st. Day at Littlehampton. On the way home Tony entertains another boy for over one hour in the coach. I am not near enough to hear the story he is telling, but he is gesticulating, and using different voices. By the other boy's attitude the story must be vivid and amusing. There is no flagging in Tony's inventiveness or dramatic expression until the coach stops.

September 5th. Tony has grown very pleasant and co-operative. He is obviously intelligent, and I believe him to be out of place in our school. Yet he wishes to stay, and has no desire to get on well enough to go back to ordinary school. He is having a trial in a different class again, but often comes to ask if he may come back to my room. His teacher reports that he is very hard working and interested, not only in reading but in each subject and activity. She reports his difficulties in P.T. Seems to have no idea how to jump over a rope, however low. (This replacing of Tony in a class is rather too soon, but as I am going on a year's leave, it is necessary to break into his experimental treatment.)

September 6th. Medical exam.: Mental Age $8\frac{2}{12}$. Chronological Age $8\frac{11}{12}$. I.Q. 92. This result is not surprising, but leads to difficulties. Tony is obviously unready for an ordinary school. He is only just beginning to co-operate with other children, and he is still liable to become withdrawn and to moon about absent-mindedly. There is obviously some psychological difficulty, and I request that he may be recommended for psychological treatment before he returns to an ordinary school. To send him back as he is at present, would be to court disaster both to his education (he has so much ground to make up) and to the hope of solving his emotional problems.

October. I am trying to arrange to spend some time with my 'maladjusted' group during my year's absence. Apart from this Tony will have to work in a class, where he is now settling well and working satisfactorily.

He is given extra opportunities of working in the mime groups, and the teacher of mime reports that he enters into his part and 'lives' it very well. He asked for the part of Rumpelstiltskin which he interprets excellently, using his own words (when speech is required) quite spontaneously.

November 1950. Case conference on Tony's case. Decision— Tony is to attend for three or four sessions weekly a special class for maladjusted children with school background unchanged. Later, it is hoped that, though he will continue in the maladjusted class, he will be able to attend ordinary school for remaining sessions.[1]

[1] July 1952. Tony is now a well-adjusted, interested member of his class. He shows no sign of being withdrawn, and he is normal in his social relationships. Next term he is returning to an ordinary school. (I.Q. now appears to be 100.)

Chapter VII

ACTIVITIES IN THE SPECIAL E.S.N. SCHOOL

As we have already noted, there must be a great deal of free play and creative activity in the junior special school. The admission class should be run entirely as a nursery class, using playground and classroom freely as in a nursery school, and there should be a nursery assistant to help in supervision and hygiene. Whether, however, it is desirable to run the whole school on a full programme of free activity is more doubtful.

Mentally handicapped children lack the lively curiosity and the eagerness to experiment, to discover and to learn, which is so characteristic of the normal child. The 'activity school' has been devised to surround normal children with an environment which will stimulate these qualities. Will freedom to experiment within such an environment prove equally stimulating and equally useful to a mentally handicapped child? To a great extent I think it may, provided that there is very careful supervision which is capable of becoming direction when necessary. Our children will enjoy activity for its own sake, and such enjoyment will help to rouse them from their lethargy, but they are less likely than normal children to learn from their activities—and this is where we must be ready to give definite instructions. It is doubtful whether they would, if left perfectly free, choose apparatus which involved effort—for example, they would be much more likely to pull a truck round and round the playground than to choose apparatus which would lead them to reading. If we leave them alone to experiment, it is doubtful whether their powers of reasoning would be sufficiently developed to lead them to a general rule from a number of particular cases. For example, I once asked a senior girl to see whether the milkman had been. She came back saying she did

CREATIVE ACTIVITY

not know. I said, 'Is the crate there?' 'Yes' was the reply. 'The milk crate is there. Has the milkman been?' She still could not reply. I asked one after another. Some said 'Yes', some said 'No', and some just did not know. I asked privately of those who said he had been, *why* they thought he had. Only two could give the right reason. That was with a class of E.S.N. girls aged fourteen to sixteen years. From this and many similar experiences I have come to believe that these children could continue to experiment throughout their school life without profiting much, unless guidance and direction are given. They would be very happy with plenty of apparatus, but many would simply play with it and would fail to progress.

Yet free activity is so very valuable that we must have it. I would suggest as a workable compromise, the following division of time for all who have passed out of the admission class:

15 minutes daily for P.T. and games. This introduces a certain amount of directed and organized classwork.
40 minutes daily for music and movement, including mime. This is chiefly free expression work and is an outlet for emotion, and a training in social co-operation.
60 minutes daily activity and experiment based on reading and number. This is individual choice within set limits, or guided individual or group work.

The remainder of the day is spent in free play or in creative activity (free or guided according to the need).

During the period of activity in reading and number, the children are required to settle down quietly and to work with apparatus which has been prepared with a bias towards the basic subjects. There is a large selection to choose from—toys to label, measure or buy; the house which forms a centre of interest for pre-reading activities; table games involving counting; shopping; weighing; group activites, for example, making a baker's shop with cakes and loaves modelled and painted, and having to be labelled, priced, weighed and bought. Where there are facilities for cooking this is an even more joyful activity. Details of the experimental work in reading and number are given in the appropriate sections.

By means of free play and creative work, group activities, organized lessons (for example, P.T.), and guided experimental work in reading and number, we hope to be able to satisfy the whole developing personality of the E.S.N. child. His need for security, for being wanted and accepted, his need for solitary and for social play, his urge to express himself, to play out his problems, to create and construct, together with his need to acquire simple skills and gradually to co-operate with others in social activities—all these must be satisfied. While we recognize his need for freedom of expression, we also keep in mind his need for help, support and control, at the same time trying to help him gradually to develop, within the limits of his own capacity, self-reliance, self-control and stability.

Creative Activity

In the creative work as in all the work in this type of school, two main ideas must be kept in mind.

1. The E.S.N. child's need for self-expression and his joy in creative work.
2. His lack, or partial lack, of the ability to progress without definite guidance and control.

A great deal here depends upon the individual child. I have known children who will, if left entirely free, produce varied and interesting work over a long period, using media of different kinds. Others will make one successful attempt, and will simply try to reproduce their first effort over and over again. Without guidance or direction they will not move on, and will eventually become bored and will give up effort altogether. Others, left alone, will have no ideas at all to express, and will

CREATIVE ACTIVITY

be driven to idleness, bad behaviour, or a sort of depressed laziness.

The first child should be allowed to work in his own way until he asks for help. It is not wise as a rule even to offer suggestions and advice. He has his own problems to work out, and advice only confuses him.

The second child needs suggestion and even direction when he begins to live on his past successes.

The third child needs to be guided at the beginning and gradually helped to stand upon his own feet, always remembering that painting or modelling, or constructive work, may not be the medium in which he finds self-expression. In such cases some other activity, for example, cleaning the pets' cages, gardening, etc., may be substituted.

I would suggest that all these needs can best be satisfied by including art, clay modelling, constructive work in cardboard, etc., gardening, pet-keeping, handwork, and needlework under the name of free creative activity, and spending the greater part of each afternoon, except for the music and mime period, in this way. The children then can choose their medium of expression, and individually can be guided or left free as they need.

With top junior E.S.N. children I would not include playing with toys, sand, etc., in this period, although I would give plenty of opportunity for such play at other times. The E.S.N. child is rather inclined to choose the easiest path, and it is quite likely that a child who has real talent in art, would spend day after day emptying sand quite aimlessly from one vessel to another without showing any further ambition. I knew one E.S.N. boy who was too lazy even to play with a toy. He would attempt nothing at all which involved any effort, and we began to doubt his educability. When he was made to exert himself he gradually appeared brighter mentally, and is now an excellent worker. It is essential that these children should not be allowed to sink into a kind of mental slumber, and because of this tendency on their part, we have in many cases to supply the incentive and the dynamic force until their own supply has become 'warmed up'.

For the art and constructive work, large sheets of paper, large brushes and powder paint should be supplied, together with clay, plasticine, cardboard, waste materials, etc. Other groups might choose potato cuts, raffia work, brightly coloured stitchery on hessian or canvas, cut paper work, puppet making and puppet plays, making and using properties for dramatic work, papier mâché, or pottery. As others will be gardening, pet-keeping, etc., the groups will be very small and the teacher will be able to help and direct those who need guidance, while those who really have something to express and who wish to be left alone, can be sent to work in the hall, where they will have space and freedom for their work.

As the children grow older it may sometimes be necessary, instead of allowing freedom of choice, to substitute a guided lesson in one of these aspects of creative activity, and no child will be harmed by having to join in it. We are preparing children for life, and we must help them to accept the fact that it is sometimes necessary to undertake a task which we have not chosen, and to work under external direction. When they have the social maturity to accept the group ideal, loyalty to the group, and to the teacher as group leader, must sometimes take the place of free choice and individual action. In our creative activity we give the opportunity for the individual to express himself within the group, and for the small group to express itself in co-operative work, while in the occasional guided lesson the individual takes direction, as a member of the group, from the group leader. It is hardly necessary to add that the success of this whole scheme depends upon the relationship established between the children and the staff, and their feeling of 'belonging' together, as group members whose functions may be different but whose aims are identical.

One form of directed work, which used to be very common in special schools, I would definitely cut out. That is the repetitive type of handwork—weaving on cardboard looms, etc. Such work is boring, largely purposeless, affords little opportunity for self-expression, and it lulls the child into the very state of lethargy from which we are trying to rouse him. All the work, whether directed or free, should be a medium of expression.

This has been abundantly clear in our art work. The children from the earliest ages are given opportunities for free and undirected expression. Gradually their interests begin to emerge—aeroplanes, cars, shipwrecks, etc. One boy has shown great interest in and observation of, factories and works, underground trains, buses and street scenes. He is feeling his way towards perspective in his pictures of gas-works, an underground train coming out of a tunnel and other pieces of perfectly free expression. Another showed his interest in skeletons and tortures, and his preoccupation with horrors and death. Another has shown varied interests fed by radio programmes and the cinema. Regression to infantile emotional impulses is usually treated by a period of free expression, so that the problem is worked out and the child is liberated. This use of free creative work is more fully described in the section on 'Misfits', but not only the misfits but all the children have plenty of opportunity of expressing their difficulties in this way.

In these days one feels no need to apologize for giving plenty of 'free expression', but one feels rather outmoded in advocating also directed or guided work. It is so easily interpreted as 'imposing adult standards' upon the child. On the other hand, when we find a child of four years 'expressing herself freely' upon the piano, we do not imagine that she will be able to express herself as a pianist at the age of twenty if she is left to develop entirely upon her own lines and no adult musical standards are imposed. So she is 'taught' music, she has to practise scales and exercises, or her talent will be frustrated.

We do not expect to make artists of our children by introducing guided lessons, but rather to put into their hands a more satisfactory medium of expression. So, in addition to the perfectly free art work, we introduce an occasional guided lesson, through which we hope to put our own experience at the service of the children. The guided lesson consists in:

1. A given subject, suggested by the children, or if no reasonable suggestions are forthcoming, by the teacher.
2. A discussion of the subject, the use of the medium, e.g. how colour *may* be laid on, how light shines on water, etc.
3. The teacher makes a word picture of the subject chosen. This is chiefly in order that the children may learn to work from the verbal picture to the concrete expression. Their usual path is from the concrete, but if they can learn to form a visual image from a word picture, this will help them in their reading comprehension.
4. The children begin their picture, and are perfectly free to express the subject in any way they choose. Advice and suggestions are offered, however, when necessary.

That this guided lesson is truly self-expression is plain from the very varied work produced in it, e.g. subject given was 'Boats seen through a window'. Two expressions of this subject may be described:

1. A great white-sailed barge is reflected in the water. The sun is setting and the water is broken up into ripples of red and gold. The whole is seen through a closed sash-window. The colours are bright and happy and the whole scene is gay.
2. An open casement window shows a dawning knowledge of perspective. A bowl of yellow crocuses stands on the window-sill, on which also the hand of the beholder is resting. Outside small boats are floating on the dark water. The main colours are dark blue and grey, and the whole effect is of night and mystery.

CREATIVE ACTIVITY

The experience gained in these guided lessons is incorporated in the perfectly free work, which thus shows a steady improvement in technique. This interchange of free expression and guidance extends to all the creative work, needlework, pattern making, potato cut printing, puppetry, dramatic work and to practically every form of activity which we use in the school.

Among the other forms of expression work, the most important is music and mime. It is essential that this work should grow out of the interests and enjoyment of the children. I think it a mistake to impose adult standards of soft and beautiful singing upon children who are longing to express their upsurging emotions in song. Singing should, in my opinion, grow out of rhythmic movement, and wordless singing as an expression of the joy of movement should be encouraged. The children need also some songs with words they can understand, enjoy, and dramatize, from the nursery rhyme stage onward. But I think that enjoyment should not be sacrificed to what we adults consider a pure sweet tone. Children love to sing out and should be allowed to do so. Just as we have the guided lesson in other art forms however, I think that each singing lesson should include one or more songs which are sung softly and sweetly, according to the adult idea of music, and some really beautiful music should be listened to in respectful silence. So taste, as we understand it, can be built up and will gradually take the place of the enjoyment of rhythmic noise. While music still means rhythmic noise to the children, the percussion band is most valuable. Our children prefer such music as the 'Gnomes Dance' from Peer Gynt to simpler works for percussion. Their pure joy in the music, rhythm and noise is a delight to see.

The rhythmic movement is perhaps the most important part of the music lesson, for here the child's appreciation of beauty is expressed emotionally. It is essential that only beautiful music should be used for this, and the movement and mime should be quite free and individual. Out of this will develop quite naturally the miming of stories to music. We have found this a most valuable means of emotional expression, of social training, and of developing spontaneous speech. When we first had a visiting music teacher, the 'misfits' were formed into a special mime group, and the progress made through this means in personal and social adjustment was so great that opportunities for mime were extended to all the children in the school. The miming is done to music, but the children are free to clarify their meaning by using speech. This has to be introduced in the first place by the teacher, but once the children get the idea they are very quick to develop it. It is often necessary to tell them when to speak and what to say, but later they use their own words quite spontaneously. Children who were too shy to speak find no difficulty now in using speech during the mime. As a means of language training it is invaluable.

There are children who have no wish to use art, craft or music and mime as a means of expression. They should not, as a rule, be forced, but should be allowed to discover their own medium—odd jobs, perhaps, gardening, building, woodwork. What is important is that each child should have the benefit of the 'loosening' effect of self-expression. Release from tension, and an outlet for emotional impulses are urgent needs of these children, and given plenty of opportunities for expression on their mental-age level, they should the more easily build up a stable and integrated personality. These art forms are chiefly valuable in that they provide a safety-valve for these children whose mental age is so far below their physical age, while at the same time they provide a means of sublimating unacceptable emotional impulses and directing them towards social ends.

Language and Reading

Comparatively few children in the junior E.S.N. school are sufficiently mature to read, and most of our work is with language and pre-reading activities. The mental ages range

LANGUAGE AND READING

from two and a half to eight years. Reading readiness is rarely attained before the mental age of six and a half years, and to attempt to teach reading before the children have sufficient maturity and experience is simply a waste of time. The number of children whose mental ages range from six and a half to eight years is usually rather small in a junior school— perhaps a fifth of the whole number may progress to this level before they move to a secondary school. Those whose mental ages are below six and a half, even though they may actually be ten or eleven years old, can be helped to reach reading readiness in the junior school, but their start in formal reading must be made in the secondary school.

In the junior school, then, the chief emphasis will be on language, vocabulary, and pre-reading activities rather than on the actual skill of reading, though this will be taught where circumstances permit.

Training in the use of speech has been discussed elsewhere, but it must be emphasized that there cannot be too much conversation and discussion. The children must be encouraged to express their ideas and to communicate with one another through language. This involves much talking throughout the day, but talking must be allowed. The development of speech in natural and accidental situations, without tension or strain, is immeasurably more valuable than a silent classroom. By talking with the teacher and listening to her, the children increase their vocabulary, and find a model whose speech they may imitate. For this reason it is most important that the teacher's speech and manner should be worthy of imitation. A teacher who shouts cannot expect children with quiet, pleasant speaking voices. One who addresses children discourteously will find her class discourteous to others. Fascinating as current slang may be, the teacher should never use it. Her standard of English must remain high, and she must never talk down to the children either by adopting baby language, or by taking over the popular slang of the moment.

At each stage in the junior school as much time as possible should be devoted to the telling of stories. The children who have hardly begun to speak will try to join in, for example, 'Who's been sitting on my chair?' and similar well-known passages. As soon as they are able children should retell stories, dramatize them, and generally use words as often as possible. It is hardly necessary to mention all the opportunities the children should have for talking—about weather, nature specimens, the pets, news, pictures on the wall, pictures and toys, etc. which they bring to school, about educational visits, about features of their environment, about games, lessons, school milk and the milkman's work, the classroom fire and the miner's work—the openings are endless. Speech is also helped through singing, puppets, mime, dramatic work—and even through learning jingles and nursery rhymes.

All this speech work has a direct bearing on reading readiness. It increases the vocabulary, helps children to choose words according to their meaning, and increases their ability to receive an idea which is expressed verbally. It is useless to attempt to teach reading until the vocabulary warrants it, and reading will be a mechanical meaningless thing until children have learned to associate words with their meaning. Work with language must begin when the child first enters the school, although it must, of course, be quite informal and entirely without strain or tension. This work is of paramount importance, and is the basis of all our work in reading and of most of our work in other subjects. It is impossible to rate it too highly.

The more definite pre-reading activities should grow out of the general activities as the child shows readiness. Labelling toys, window, door, flowers in the nature corner, pets' cages, etc., can be done afresh each day. Notices about the school, 'Please shut the door', or over the wash-basins, 'Wash your hands', will help to form a very early concept of the use of reading for everyday purposes. A centre of interest, for example a house for the younger children, or a Red Indians' encampment

LANGUAGE AND READING

for those slightly older will provide endless opportunities for learning names and labelling objects, and for making stories which can be written up on the wall and read back by the children. Word matching and word and picture matching grows easily from these centres of interest, and the resourceful teacher will be able to harness a great deal of the work of the school in the cause of reading interest.

As the children become more mature the desire to read should gradually develop. Usually this desire will come, provided that the ground has been well prepared. The child has discovered that the ability to read has its uses in the everyday world of reality. To be able to read where a bus is going, or to read out a shopping list, or to read street notices is a skill worth having. He has also discovered that reading is the door into a magic world of stories. Comprehension has always been an integral part of our work in language, but, although an idea of the usefulness and romance of reading has already been built up, I think it worth while to emphasize these points before formal reading is actually started. There are many ways of doing this, but I suggest two types of activity as possible means to this end. One is based on reality, and is a somewhat limited exploration of the environment, and the other points the way to stories through reading.

The first is based on the experience of travelling to school, and through this a more thorough exploration of the environment could be made if desired. Special school children usually travel some distance to school, and come from various directions. I would suggest that each child in a small group should have a small bus to label with the number of the bus he travels on. A small—and very simple—model of the school should be placed upon the floor, and roads laid out from the school to the home of each child in the group. The buses should then be placed on their routes, and the main roads labelled. Traffic lights, police points, road signs, etc., should be placed in position and labelled, together with the main bus stops. Visits should, if possible, be made to each point, and the children should look out for street names, etc. So each child learns to recognize the buses, street names and street notices of his own neighbourhood. Important buildings can be added and their use discussed. 'Safety First' posters will provide extra reading material, and the children can paint and letter posters advertising transport. Nothing elaborate need be attempted in model making. The purpose is to underline one of the uses of reading, rather than to produce a grand model. When the bus routes are known, trains and their stations can be introduced, and then the river with its ships, wharves and factories. The model will spread all over the floor and will have to be put away each afternoon, but the children will gain very much by having to put it out and arrange points and labels correctly each day. A full environmental exploration could be incorporated into this—visits to fire station, trip up the river by river bus, visits to the bus garage, to local factories—as much as can be arranged. These visits are more difficult to arrange for junior than for secondary age children however. Our chief purpose at the moment, though, is to interest the children in recognizing local place-names, street names, notices, and the names of important buildings in the neighbourhood, in order that they may see that reading ability is useful in everyday travelling.

The other suggestion is a means of connecting reading with stories through dramatic work. Sometimes we use puppets, and sometimes the children act.

(*a*) Using puppets. Punch and Judy Show.
  1. Children sing 'Punchinello'.
  2. Card is shown 'Punch is dancing with Judy'. Children read the card and show its meaning by working puppets. Then a child reads the card aloud. This is continued so as to make a short Punch and Judy story (about five sentences).

LANGUAGE AND READING

3. The sentences have been illustrated, duplicated and bound together into books. These books are given to the children. They recognize the sentences they have already learned, connect them with the pictures and the show they have seen, and recognize the fact that reading ability means the ability to read a story.

(*b*) Children acting, e.g. 'Three Little Pigs'.

1. Cards are printed and children hang them round their neck. e.g. Little pig (three cards), bad wolf. The house cards are in the shape of a house and were made by the children. They show the wood, straw or brick houses and are labelled 'house of wood', etc.
2. Card is shown, 'A little pig built a house of wood.' Children act it. Another card, 'The bad wolf blew it down.' Children act it. Third card, 'He ate the little pig.' Children act it. The value of this is that reading and comprehension must go together in order that the acting may be done. So through the whole story of the three houses, ending with the safety and happiness of the third little pig.
3. Duplicated sentences are bound into a book, which the children can read immediately.

By this means, reading is connected with the unfolding of a story, and every word is seen to have meaning. At the same time reading, comprehension and action are almost simultaneous, and reading is connected in the child's mind with enjoyment rather than drudgery. Many other stories lend themselves also to this treatment.

It is probable that when the children find that stories can be read in books, they will begin to frequent the reading corner. Suitable books are those with coloured pictures with a short simple sentence under each. If these are difficult to obtain they can be made after the manner of scrap-books, care being taken that the vocabulary is properly controlled and repeated. Children should also make their own books, with their own pictures and sentences. Some of these books should be made from pictures cut from magazines, etc., and some from pictures drawn by the child. Individual and class libraries can be built up in this way. From the reading corner interest, children will begin really to read, coming to ask the teacher or a more advanced child any word they do not recognize.

At this stage the reading book and real individual reading lessons should be introduced. Training, so far, has been on whole word and sentence recognition, and phonic word building should not, as a rule, be introduced yet. We have found the Janet and John readers among the most suitable, and good books are now being produced for the older children who are longing to adventure away from the ordinary world into a world of Red Indians, etc. For these older children it will usually be necessary to make supplementary readers based on the adventures of pirates and other 'heroes'. Reading must still be based on activity, and a centre of interest affords the most useful opportunities for such activities. Work books and picture dictionaries are most useful, especially as the children are now longing to do real school work such as their friends in 'ordinary schools' are doing. There is a dignity about making a dictionary and using a work book that never extends to such activities as word and picture matching!

Mentally handicapped children progress very slowly, and when they have read the Introductory Book of whatever series they are using, they are rarely ready for Book I. So Book I should not immediately be followed by Book II. Several books of each grade, using practically the same vocabulary, are needed. These must be very carefully selected, but it is usually possible to find books which will 'fit in' with whatever series we have first chosen. As an alternative supplementary books can be made.

In the junior school we can rarely hope to find a reading age of more than seven to eight years, and we shall find many whose attainment falls far below this level. Some have what appears to be a special reading disability, and will probably leave school at sixteen years old having a reading age of perhaps six years. In some schools it has been the practice to press forward in the mechanical recognition of words, and children actually can learn to read the words without having the slightest comprehension of what they are reading. So deeply engrained is the habit of reading without comprehension that I doubt whether such children, even though they finally attain perhaps a nine- or ten-year-old standard in mechanical reading, will ever read a book for pleasure. In such cases the skill will not be retained after school-leaving age, and the hours spent in acquiring it will have been largely wasted. I have such a case in mind. Margaret came to us at the age of ten years old having already some skill in mechanical reading. In June 1950 her mental age was 6 years 6 months and her mechanical reading age 6 years 4 months. Yet she would read in her work book 'Paint the house red' and then would have no idea what to do. The words read had not the remotest connexion in her mind with reality. The reading rather constituted a barrier between words and their meaning. If a teacher had said 'Paint the house red', Margaret could have done so without difficulty. Once she had read the words, her teacher had the utmost difficulty in getting her to see that the house had to be painted red. Such reading I regard as useless and a complete waste of time, for no foundations had been laid.

In the junior school we must concentrate on laying deep and strong foundations of language, vocabulary, and pre-reading activities. If we are able in individual cases to start the reading also, we do so very thankfully, and the child is able to read before he enters his secondary school. If in other individual cases the child is not sufficiently mature to begin formal reading before he leaves us for the secondary school, we must be content to have laid foundations upon which, in due time, another will be able to build firmly and securely.

At the present time, each of the twenty-three children in our top class (ages nine to eleven) has built up a reading interest, and is able to read at least the introductory book of the Janet and John series with understanding and enjoyment, and most are going forward quite quickly. We feel that we have gained by concentrating on pre-reading activities for a very long period before attempting any definite teaching of reading. The children have written sentences under their own pictures, and have been encouraged to make a series of pictures which tell a connected story. Many of these have been inspired by Captain Marvel and other film heroes, but others have written of the Crusaders, the jungle, explorers, pirates, the Normans, cave men, prehistoric animals, and other interests which they have acquired through the very frequent story lessons, the cinema, television, wireless, museums, and the picture books in our book corner. In the midst of all this we gradually introduce word games, and all the words for the introductory book are learned in this way.

No child is given the first book until he can immediately recognize every word in it. While he is reading the first book, he is being taught the words for the second, and so on. Until he has a good reading vocabulary he is never given a book until he has learned all the words in it. This necessitates constant individual work and testing, and carefully kept records, but to the children it does not seem dull. They are most enthusiastic about it, and are glad to have the words they do not know written down to learn for 'homework' (which they love to have). This concentration on words does not mean that we neglect the sentence method. We use this word technique only for our graded series of reading books. When a child gets his first book, he is able to read it at once without any difficulty. The story and the pictures are discussed with the teacher, and his interest in the book is maintained by much expression work based on it. As we have waited for the child to become ready for the experience of reading, we reap the benefit in this enthusiasm and consequent success. There is no time of failure and discouragement. The child has not become bored or disheartened. He has reached the point where he really sees the use of reading and wants to learn, and enjoys every moment of it. When the correct emotional attitude has been built up the chief difficulty has been side-tracked, and the child goes forward at an amazing speed for his level of intelligence. Reading becomes a pleasure, not an ordeal, and a skill which is pleasurable is more likely to be retained after school-leaving age than one which is associated with boredom and failure.

Even so, however, there may be some children who are not ready to begin formal reading at primary-school age, and we must not be discouraged if lack of maturity or experience, the memory of past failures in the ordinary school, or some special reading disability should hold them back so that they cannot make a start. It would, of course, be much better for such children if they could remain in the school where the foundations of reading are being laid, so that they might benefit from continuity of method.

Unfortunately, however, in some districts continuity of teaching method in reading and in other subjects has to be broken by the transfer at the physical age of eleven, which may be a mental age of anything from five and a half to eight plus. The setback to a mentally handicapped child is much more upsetting than in the case of normal children whose mental age is at least level with their physical age. It is my belief that mentally handicapped children need to continue throughout their school life in one stable background, in a calm, controlled and yet free school climate. To transplant them when they have begun to adjust themselves to a certain environment, is to undermine a great deal of the work the school should be doing. Unfortunately the policy is to provide junior and senior schools in order that there may be 'secondary education for all'. In my opinion it is a thousand pities to sacrifice the developmental welfare of

Number

It is essential that number, in a school for mentally handicapped children, should be based on the interests and the needs of their everyday life. All else should be firmly excluded from the scheme of work, for, to pursue the subject for its own sake is not only useless, but positively harmful. The number needs of these children—even when they leave school—are very few indeed. I would assess them as follows:

1. Ability to count, and to add and subtract reasonably small numbers (i.e. only such numbers as can be added or subtracted mentally). They have no need of hundreds—in fact number up to 50 is an over-generous estimate of their needs. They may need to be able to multiply and divide small sums *mentally*, but will have little occasion to write such sums. It is useful to add and subtract 'on paper', as well as mentally, for scoring games, etc. I would not encourage any more work than this in 'pure number' up to the school-leaving age.
2. Money. This is, and always will be, their chief use for number, and I would do as much work as possible, mentally and with coins, in calculating costs, change, etc., writing bills, laying out pocket-money, suggested lay-outs of weekly wages, etc. In the junior school great facility should be gained in dealing with pence and halfpence up to one shilling and in the secondary school this should be extended within the limits of the individual child's capacity.
3. Length. Much experimental work in measuring will help them in their craft work, both in the junior and secondary school.
4. Capacity and Weight. Practical experience in weighing and measuring capacity will be necessary for cookery, etc.

NUMBER

5. Time. It is essential for every child to learn to tell the time during his school life.

As the curriculum is based on the few simple *needs* of the children, so the method of teaching must be based upon such abilities as they possess. Mentally handicapped children rarely have normal powers of reasoning, nor much capacity for abstract thought. Our methods must, then, be practical, and our best approach is through activity and experiment. In the very early stages general activities can be used, and number concepts will, we hope, gradually grow from this free play and experiment. As we go on we must gradually modify these methods and adapt them to the children we have to deal with. There are two points which it is important to recognize. In the first place mentally handicapped children have rarely that ardent curiosity and the desire to understand and learn about their environment, which characterize the normally intelligent child. Left alone their experimental activity would tend to degenerate into mere 'messing about'. They need more direction and supervision, and more external stimuli—they must be encouraged, or even forced, to engage in purposeful activities, rather than be left free to by-pass these in favour of effortless occupations. For example, a boy who enjoyed sand play was left free to pursue his own activities and he chose to spend day after day, over a long period, in pouring sand from one vessel to another, without change or progress. External urge directed his energies into more purposeful channels, and he has become a solid and excellent worker, who, when last tested (Burt Mental Arithmetic Tests), was up to his mental age in attainment. Many examples of this kind can be given. Secondly, mentally handicapped children, engaged in experimental activity, are unlikely to extract a number law from their experimental work. For example, during water or sand play they may use capacity measures, filling a quart measure from pint measures again and again. They will enjoy the activity, but very rarely will they come to the conclusion that 2 pints equal 1 quart. I remember seeing a girl weighing beads. The scale did not go down when she poured some beads in, so she took more beads from the pan—again and again—and neither she nor the group round her saw that *more* not *fewer* beads were needed. Even the activity itself then, they may fail to carry out properly, and how much greater is the failure to draw the correct conclusion from it. Experimental work is indeed necessary, and without it number work is absolutely meaningless. The old number work with mentally handicapped children, in which they did pages of 'sums', was a waste of the teacher's and children's time, and the taxpayers' money. Yet the experimental work may prove an equal waste, unless the children are definitely taught to do the work correctly, and how to apply it, and what conclusions to draw from it.

For these two reasons, their lack of drive, and their inability to formulate a law from their experimental work, mentally handicapped children need very definite help and teaching within the framework of experimental activity. I have found that the best solution of these problems, within my experience, is to set aside a definite time during the day for activities based on number, from the time that the children reach the mental age of five and a half to six. This period really is for activity, not for formal number, but the child is not free, for example, to pull a truck round the yard—he must engage in some number work or experiment, while the teacher definitely teaches groups or individuals, helping them to perform the weighing, measuring, etc., correctly, and to draw the right conclusion from it.

Having explained the appearance on our time-table of a period of activity based on number, we can trace the various stages of number work in our junior school:

The admission class (ages five to seven. Mental Ages two and a half to four and a half years) is run entirely as a nursery class, and from the general free play we hope that a number sense will gradually be formed. The most definite work at this stage is with the nursery school educational apparatus—nested beakers for size, posting-box for shape, pegs and squares for recognizing quantities (1 peg, 2 pegs, 3 pegs, etc.), peg boards for many and few, building bricks with their numerous uses, threading beads, etc. But most of the day is spent in free play during which number ideas will be encouraged by the teacher, for example, counting in many games; heavy and light things, especially in water play, and in lifting various objects; long and short, large and small, many and few, will come into building and many other activities; tall and short children will be noted, big and small shoes; full and empty noted in sand and water play and first ideas on capacity will be formed. Time concepts will gradually emerge, especially if a routine is carefully kept —play-time—dinner-time—rest-time—milk-time—music-time —story-time—home-time. At this early stage practical experience of length, time, space, capacity, weight, etc., will be gained during the general activities, and will simply be underlined by the teacher.

The next stage is the substitution of a short period of activity *based on number* for part of the general activity. This begins round about the mental age of five and a half, when the chronological age is between seven and a half and ten years. Among the number activities which may be used are the following:

1. For the recognition of number symbols:

   (a) Number tops, fishpond game, bagatelle and ring boards (numbers altered to bring them within children's range) skittles, and any other scoring games. Number lotto (later stages).

   (b) Small toys and objects placed next to number symbols, e.g. 2 cars, 3 dolls, 5 balls, etc. Toys, etc., are more attractive than counters and have more correlation with reality as the child sees it.

2. Length, height, width, etc., comparative rather than actual measurements, but where a measuring stick is used it should

be of a standard length, so that in the later stages it can lead to real measurement.

(a) Project work, especially building projects which involve much measuring.
(b) Comparing sizes of children, and objects of various kinds.
(c) Families of dolls, bears, etc. (or picture cut-outs), arranged in order of height.
(d) Measuring curtains for wendy house, fitting clothes to various-sized dolls, bedding to various dolls' beds, etc.
(e) Weight—weighing various objects to find heavier (comparative weights), playing shops, etc.
(f) Money used for shopping, post office, etc., pennies and halfpence (cardboard). Stamps and bus tickets are useful here.
(g) Capacity—sand and water play with standard capacity measures.
(h) Time—clock faces (individual) on which children can show certain times (hours only), 10—lesson-time, 11—play-time, 12—dinner-time, 1—lesson-time again, 2—play-time, 3—home-time, etc.
(i) Quick practice in mental calculation with groups (practice based on the practical work the group or individual is doing).

The teacher may wish to incorporate all this number activity into a project, but this depends entirely upon the abilities and leanings of individual teachers. It must be remembered, though, that projects call for more co-operative work than some of these children are yet ready for. Some—or many—are still at the stage of individual activity, rather than at that of co-operative effort.

In the later stages in the junior school, mental ages six to seven, chronological ages nine to eleven, children will learn a great deal from their 'jobs' about the school—giving out milk, getting right numbers of knives, forks, etc., and setting tables. Experimental work in number will be carried farther:

Money. Shopping with coins, using sixpence and shilling and other coins according to individual ability. Making bills with easy sums, thus introducing written arithmetic. (See below—'Reading and number activity.') Counting up dinner money. Shopping in real shops—buying oats, straw, sawdust for guinea pigs, etc.

Weight. Shop play using real weights, and gradually learning ounces, ¼ lb., ½ lb., 1 lb., and their relative values.

Capacity. Sand and water play with capacity measures. Giving out milk—3 bottles equals 1 pint. (See below—'Activity based on school milk.')

Length. Measuring as before, but using 12-inch ruler, yard measure, etc. Measuring and planning for needlework and handwork.

Time. Time telling with individual clock faces, and old clocks and watches.

Written Arithmetic. Before they leave the junior school children should be ready to do a small amount of written arithmetic, but whether they actually are ready or not, they *need* it. They are living in a world where it is humiliating not to be able to 'do sums'. Their parents and friends set the standard, and the child feels a need to live up to his environment. A very little will save his self-respect, and easy addition and subtraction sums (units only), as well as bills or money sums should be done.

In the earlier stages the children have been scoring mentally, or jotting down scores and adding them, and out of all the experimental number work a fairly good (E.S.N.!) standard of mental arithmetic will have been evolving. Part of the number activity period should be given to quick mental work, and number practice and drills. Then, when 'sums' are started there will be little difficulty, and, in many cases, it will be unnecessary to use counters, etc., to count by. Written work is comparatively unimportant, and what importance it has is very largely psychological, so that emphasis must still be on experimental work, and mental arithmetic. It is useless to introduce any written sums which involve larger numbers than can be worked mentally, and I would ruthlessly cut out all such work from E.S.N. schools, junior or secondary. At the end of the junior school period there will be a wide variation of individual attainment, so that though group co-operation can be used at times, the work must remain very largely individual. The amount of arithmetic learned will necessarily be very small, limited as it is by the capacity and needs of the child, but qualitatively the deviation from the normal achievement should not be very noticeable in most cases. The chief difference between the achievement of the mentally handicapped child and the normal child of equal *mental* age, is the difficulty with which the E.S.N. child applies his experimental work to a new situation. There is also, in many cases, a lag in arithmetic age behind mental age, owing either to special disability or late ascertainment, in which case the child finds it difficult to make up his past failures in a short time. He may catch up with himself before the age of sixteen, but it will be a very slow process.

To summarize, we hope that the child will leave the junior school with considerable experimental knowledge of the use of weight, capacity, length and money, and will be well on the way towards telling the time. In addition he should be able to do written sums in addition and subtraction of units, and add money, with halfpence, to one shilling or more according to his ability. The brightest may be able to do rather more, and the dullest will probably do none of these things. Yet brightest and dullest alike will have a vivid enjoyment of the subject, which is more than some of us, who were taught by the traditional methods, have ever had.

A Reading and Number Activity

This begins as an individual activity. A number of toys and other small objects are labelled and put in a tin (an aluminium sandwich tin with a coloured lid is very attractive and useful for this purpose). We made twenty-six different tins of objects, e.g.

1. Empty shampoo bottle, comb, slide, brush, mirror.
2. Screw, lock and key, bolt, oil-can, door handle.
3. Toy kettle, teapot, cup, saucer, jug, spoon.
4. Toy broom, mop, carpet-sweeper, pail, scrubbing brush.
5. Frying-pan, saucepan, colander, rolling-pin, bowl.
6. Bus, car, lorry, traffic lights, petrol pump, etc., etc.

In each tin are large cards on which the names of the objects are written. The children match the labelled objects with these name cards, and then place price tickets on them. The price tickets vary according to the individual capacity of the child. Some are for two or three pence only, some have pence and halfpence, and some have shillings and pence.

The child chooses a tin, matches the names on the labels, prices the objects, and then places the correct amount in cardboard coins beside each price label. This is his shop. He then sells two or more objects (according to his ability), and makes a bill for them. He copies the name and price of the objects, and adds the total cost, using the coins to help his calculation if he needs to. He changes his tin when he wishes. Progress from addition of pence only, to addition of shillings and pence with halfpence proceeds naturally, and little difficulty is felt, while the word matching and the writing of the names and prices help in developing the skills of reading and writing.

Although this starts as an individual activity, it would be a pity to miss the opportunity of social training which its development into a communal activity provides. So sometimes we have a market. Tins are taken by half the children, and their wares are spread on tables, labelled and priced. Each shopkeeper is given a sum of money to start with, and they are told that this sum must be handed back at the end before they check the amount they have taken for goods sold. The shoppers have, usually, a shilling to spend (saved in the bank from the milk activity. See below.) The shopkeepers make bills for what they sell, and the shoppers note their spendings in their account books. When funds are getting low a halt is called. Buyers and sellers add up their accounts, and balance them with the cash in hand. Here we get subtraction as well as addition of money. If an account does not balance, we visit the shops in turn, until the giver of wrong change is discovered.

It is most important, in this market, that a sharp eye should be kept on the giving and accepting of change, and that the accounts of each child should be correctly balanced at the end. If this is not done the thing would simply become a game without purpose, in which the children could learn wrong values of coins. The great danger of these methods is that, unless the activity of each child is very carefully supervised, the children can very easily learn what is false instead of what is true. Learning by experience is excellent, as long as we can make sure that the right things are experienced, and that the right conclusions are drawn from the experience. Unless we can make certain of these things, it is much better not to attempt to use these methods. With these safeguards, however, such an activity affords valuable opportunities for expression through speech, for training in good social manners, and for learning the skills of reading, writing and number in a natural setting and with a real purpose.

An Activity based on School Milk

Our school milk is delivered in $\frac{1}{3}$-pint bottles, and the staff buys milk in $\frac{1}{2}$-pint or pint bottles. The children are given empty bottles, large jugs, basins and funnels to experiment with. They use water to discover how may $\frac{1}{3}$-pint and how many $\frac{1}{2}$-pint bottles are needed to fill a pint bottle. A great deal of this experimental work is done and then it is followed up by mental arithmetic which uses the facts discovered by experiment.

When this has been done, we begin to appoint a weekly 'milkman'. He opens his dairy each morning after he has arranged the bottles in threes to discover how many pints he has. While the bottles are arranged in groups of three, the children build up and learn 3 times table, moving the bottles into groups of two threes, three threes, four threes, etc. They work out how many pints would be needed for 3, 6, 9, 12, etc., children, and how many children could be served from 1 pint, 2 pints, 3 pints, etc. Similar work is done with $\frac{1}{2}$-pint bottles and the table is worked out. Of course only a small amount of this work is done each day, just before the milkman actually begins to sell his milk. Then the business of buying and selling begins.

On Monday each child is given a cardboard shilling, which he puts into the 'bank'. A new banker and secretary are chosen each week. The price of a pint of milk is fixed at sixpence, and the children work out that their $\frac{1}{3}$-pint bottle would cost twopence. Each morning they visit the bank, take out twopence, and go to the dairy. Each must ask, in words, for a third of a pint of milk. The milkman gives the bottle of milk and takes twopence. Empty bottles are arranged in threes, and the number of pints actually used is immediately seen. Then the children work out the amount of money the milkman should have taken. Those who cannot do this soon learn by touching each bottle while they count twopence, fourpence, sixpence, and so on to tenpence, a shilling, etc. For amounts above a shilling they are asked how many pennies, e.g. 1s. 4d.—How many pennies would the milkman have to make 1s. 4d.? When the whole amount spent has been worked out (in twopences by counting each bottle at twopence, or in sixpences by counting groups of three at sixpence a pint) the milkman turns out his till and counts his money to see if it tallies. The secretary's work is to keep the accounts. For this purpose we have a board on which small screw hooks have been placed so that cardboard coins can be hung in full view of all. Rings sold for *passe-partout* framing can easily be fixed through the coins so that they can be hung up. (See diagram.)

When the children take their shilling to the bank on Monday morning, a cardboard shilling is hung on the hooks marked

```
              OUR   BANK

Paid in                                       Spent

 ⊗ ⊗  ○ ○  ○ ○  ○ ○      Monday         ○ ○     ○ ○
 ⊗ ⊗  ○ ○  ○ ○  ○ ○      Tuesday        ○ ○     ○ ○
                          Wednesday      ○ ○     ○ ○
                          Thursday       ○ ○     ○ ○
                          Friday         ○ ○     ○ ○

Savings

 ○ ○  ○ ○  ○ ○  ○ ○  ○ ○  ○ ○
 ○ ○  ○ ○  ○ ○  ○ ○  ○ ○
```

'Paid in'. At milk-time this is changed for twelve pennies which hang on the twelve hooks. As the children spend their twopence for milk every day, the secretary takes two pennies from 'Paid in', and hangs them under 'Spent'. The children can then see quite plainly that 1s. minus 2d.=10d., 1s. minus 4d.= 8d. etc. At the end of the week two pennies are left in the bank. These are transferred to the hooks marked 'Savings'. Children work out how many weeks it will take to save 1s. When 1s. has been saved they can take it out of the bank to spend in the market (see 'Reading and number activity' above). Money calculations grow very easily from the use of this banking account board, and we hope later on, to get each child to keep his own 'bank book'. The children would like to extend this game to school dinners, but we have not yet attempted it.

Short note on arithmetic in the secondary E.S.N. school

In the secondary school the same principles should be applied as in the junior school. Only such arithmetic as is *useful* should be taught, and this should be based upon the interests of the children and expressed through experimental activity.

Length and measurement, weight, capacity, time telling, using money, adding and subtracting easy number, can all be taught through carpentry, needlework, craftwork, cookery, shopping, scoring games, practical jobs in the school, travelling, and other activities. If a definite number period is used in addition to these practical activities, it is well to base the number, reading and English work upon a project—either an exploration of the environment, or upon a centre of interest. There is no more point in the secondary school, than in the junior school, in teaching elaborate rules for their own sake. Unless they have a practical application, and one that can be used immediately, it is simply a waste of time to teach them. Within the E.S.N. service, the junior school is the place for individual activity and experiment, working gradually towards group co-operation, while the secondary school is the place for project work, which depends so much upon social co-operative ability while leaving much scope for individual initiative and the development of qualities of leadership.

Chapter VIII

WHAT IS 'SUCCESS' IN SPECIAL SCHOOL TREATMENT?

At the age of eleven our junior school children leave us for the secondary E.S.N. school. We have given them a great deal of freedom, but what do we hope to achieve by it? What should they carry from us to their secondary school?

The first and most important work we can do in the junior school is to lay the foundations of a stable and well-integrated personality. The child should be alert and interested, and capable of adjusting himself. He should have formed interests and hobbies and have found socially acceptable outlets for his emotional impulses. The ground should have been thoroughly prepared and the seeds of the basic skills sown, even though the shoots may not yet appear above the ground. There should be a readiness about the child which makes it possible to lead him forward—he should be reaching out to wider interests and experiences which the secondary school can supply.

We who work in the junior school will never see the harvest we have sown. In personality building, social training, and skills we can only prepare the child, and lay the best foundations we can. But we have a share in the success or failure of special school treatment in the case of each child, and we can look forward and view the standards by which that success or failure must be judged. The success or failure of special school treatment for the child who is educationally sub-normal through mental handicap, can be judged by the progress made in certain directions.

The child should be helped to make the best of such capabilities as he possesses, and by steady hard work to compensate as far as possible for his disabilities. He will be given a sense of achievement through work which is within his capacity, and

WHAT IS 'SUCCESS'?

through hobbies, interests, practical jobs, etc., a sense of responsibility and a degree of self-reliance will be encouraged. Efforts will be made to widen his horizon, and to get him to be interested in his environment, instead of apathetic. The criterion by which he will be judged at school-leaving age is a social and no longer an educational one. We must help him to adjust to his environment, and to become, as far as possible, a steady, hard-working and conscientious citizen, able with adequate supervision, to support himself and manage his own affairs.

Yet I do not regard it as a school failure—necessarily—if the child is either unable to reach this standard, or if, having appeared socially efficient at the end of his school career, he regresses later. This regression may happen with a normal child, or one who has been trained in an approved school, as well as with a mentally handicapped child. With normal or delinquent children, although we spare no effort to give them a code of behaviour, moral standards and a sense of values, we yet have to recognize that they are endowed with free will, and that we cannot use it for them. God Himself respects their free will, and though He gives them a knowledge of the right way, He does not force them to walk in it. We must recognize that human beings will not necessarily walk in the ways *we* have shown them. We think we have reformed them, and when we see them turning again to their own ways we cannot bear it. In our pride we attribute their failure to ourselves, but inwardly we are also claiming the success of all the others we have trained. We appropriate to ourselves the failure of the one so that we may also appropriate the success of the others, but neither belongs to us. We have been nothing but temporary instruments used in the moulding of character for part of the child's training-time. If this is so with normal children, it is even more obviously so with our mentally handicapped children. If we are honest we must admit that throughout their school career they have never been capable of entire self-reliance and self-control. They have needed constant guidance and supervision, and we have been continually on the alert, ready to step in whenever their own abilities fail them. When they leave us for a more unsympathetic world where they have to stand alone, how difficult it is for them to keep up the standards of cleanliness, punctuality, regularity and hard work, on which we have always insisted! Unless the parents are very efficient, the child is most likely to regress when he leaves us. We have done our best and have made our little contribution towards the hope of his making good, but the final success or failure is in other hands than ours.

I would, then, suggest that special school treatment has succeeded if the child is alert, interested and co-operative, and, by and large, is working up to his full mental capacity, and if he is making good use of the very limited abilities which we know him to possess.

The school may also be considered to have succeeded if, in addition to the results noted above, the child's educational attainments have been brought more nearly up to his mental-age standard. This however must be understood of education in its widest application, and not merely of academic subjects. Reading and arithmetic will usually continue to lag behind the mental age, for several reasons. The child may enter a special school with a mental age, for example, of seven years, but his attainment in 3 R's may be nil. Usually such children have picked up nothing in the ordinary school except a deeply rooted antipathy to school subjects. This has to be broken down before any attempt at teaching them can be made. He has also a deep discouragement and lack of self-confidence, and finds it very difficult to approach work which, he believes, will almost certainly lead to failure. In addition to this, the special school child often—usually, even—has a special disability for the more intellectual subjects. It may be impossible to teach him to read at all, although most can learn some small amount of arithmetic if it is based on experimental activity. When we

WHAT IS 'SUCCESS'?

speak of educational attainments being brought up to the child's mental-age level, we must include art, handwork, and practical work of all kinds, in which case we are not setting an impossible standard. But as far as reading and arithmetic are concerned, such an ideal may be impossible, and most unfair to the child. Suppose, however, that the child has ability for these subjects, we still have to deal with his lack of groundwork. If he starts from scratch at the mental age of seven, we cannot expect that at the mental age of eight he will have a reading and arithmetic age of eight also. We must be satisfied if it creeps up very slowly, and when his mental age slows to a standstill (which often happens very early in mentally handicapped children) extra practice in these subjects during the remaining years of his school career, may possibly bring them more nearly to his mental-age standard. In many cases, if not in the majority, however, the child's disability lies chiefly in these subjects. In such cases we must not expect this result. It must be sufficient for us if the child is willing to use the very little ability he has, and we must not be surprised or discouraged if he makes very little academic progress, and never learns to read. Even our best readers are most unlikely to use the subject when they leave school. Very few will ever read even the lightest book for enjoyment. Most will thankfully discard the difficult art as soon as they leave school, and will find their pleasure in the cinema or the wireless. What they are more likely to retain is their skill in handwork, provided that the materials needed are easily obtained, and I would say that the school has not succeeded, however high the standard of academic work, unless the children have, by school-leaving age, been shown some ways of using their leisure. A love of, and considerable skill in, knitting can very easily be inculcated, and there are many other simple crafts which the children will enjoy sufficiently to continue them when they leave school. They should be taught to appreciate those radio programmes which have entertainment value. These they will use when they leave school, whereas they are more likely to discard the purely educational ones. An interest in the wireless, knitting, needlework, and other simple hobbies, may encourage them to stay in in the evenings, instead of hanging about at the street corners. A school which has taught the use of leisure, even if it has not succeeded in teaching reading and arithmetic, has not failed.

INDEX

ability, 10, 33, 37, 51, 55, 61, 72, 78, 129, 135, 142
achievement, 20, 35, 47, 55, 58, 101, 134, 140
activities, 50, 52–4, 60, 67, 71, 79, 110–39
    based on reading and number, 111–12, 121–3, 130–3, 135–9
    pre-reading, 111, 118–24, 125–6
activity, 49, 51–2, 60, 68, 129, 136, 139, 142
    creative, 78, 80, 85–109, 110–18
    directed, 110–17, 129–30
    free, 110–11
adjustment, 4, 7, 10, 11, 14, 49, 61, 63, 66–7, 76–7, 118, 127, 140–1.
    between age and mental age, 61–3
after-care, 30
anti-social tendencies, 6, 14–15, 17, 31, 34–5, 49, 51, 59, 61, 65, 73–5
art, 3, 36, 52, 54, 80, 84–7, 89–97, 99–102, 114–16
assembly, 64
attainment, 16–17, 82, 84–5, 95, 134, 142–3
    ages, 82, 95–7, 100–101, 125, 134, 142–3
attitude, 92, 100
    Christian, 8–9
    emotional, 72, 127
    materialistic, 5, 9
    other children's, 48, 53, 69, 72
    parents', 18–32, 37, 48, 50, 71, 92, 98
    secular humanist's, 8–9
    teacher's, 3, 51

background, 13, 15, 18–32, 98, 103

backwardness, causes, 12
    as a symptom, 15
behaviour problems, 2, 14, 58–9, 61–3, 74–8
    disorder, 12, 14–15, 17, 34, 57, 66–8

capacities, 7, 8, 129
capabilities, 80, 140
case studies, delinquency, 34, 37, 39, 41, 43–6
    misfits, 83–97, 97–103, 103–9
centre of interest, 111, 120, 121, 124, 139
child guidance, 12, 14, 41, 54, 66
clubs, 40, 42
community, 10, 11, 47, 49, 52, 54, 57, 58, 60, 63, 68, 74
competition, 1, 30, 58, 61, 80
confidence, 51, 55, 57, 58, 60, 68, 76, 77, 82
control, 37, 40, 42, 51, 52, 62, 63, 70, 74, 78, 79, 112
co-operation, 1, 15, 40, 47, 49, 51–4, 58–60, 63, 80–2, 112, 114, 132, 139
    development of, 83–109
    parents', 19, 23, 30
    social, 53, 54, 63, 82, 107, 111, 139

deascertainment, 16, 69, 70, 83, 97, 109
delinquency, 10, 12, 28, 33–46, 49, 67, 68, 74, 98, 103, 141
development, 2, 12–17, 48, 83, 97
    of personality, 47, 48
    psychological, 67, 70–3
    social 49, 53, 71–3, 82–103
    of speech, 12, 53, 72–3, 119
developmental ages, 13, 81, 97
discipline, 23, 24, 70, 77–8
dramatic work, 93, 97, 105, 122

education, definition, 8, 10
emotions, 36, 72, 111, 117
emotional age, 61
   disturbance, 12, 14, 66–109
   expression, 117–18
   impulses, 35, 37, 40, 63, 115, 118, 140
   problems, 14–17, 41, 54, 66–109
   problems, behaviour disorder, 12, 14, 15, 17, 34, 57, 66–8
   problems, withdrawal, 15, 49, 54, 57, 64, 73, 98–100, 103–9
   retardation, 62
   satisfaction, 6
environment, 7, 10, 12, 33, 35, 37, 42, 66, 67, 69, 73, 78, 110, 121, 127, 133, 141
experiment, 49, 52, 60, 71, 72, 78–9, 80, 81, 110, 111
   in readjustment, 83–109
   in number, 129–39, 142

failure, 2, 10, 11, 24, 60, 61, 67, 68, 71, 127, 134, 141, 142
family, 52, 63
   conditions, 18–31
   influence of, 30–1, 37, 39, 42
   size of, 18, 19
freedom, 51, 63, 70, 71, 79, 110, 112, 140
   experiments in, 83–109
free play, 36, 78, 110–14, 131

gardening, 113, 114
group, 34, 48, 49, 50, 52, 53, 54, 61, 111, 114, 134, 139

hobbies, 140, 141, 144
home conditions, 13, 18–32

ideals, 35, 36, 47, 74
idleness, 67, 113
impulses, 7, 35, 36, 37, 39, 40, 42, 47, 51, 52, 62, 63, 115
   emotional, 35, 37, 40, 63, 115, 118, 140
independence, 48, 50, 51, 57, 72

indolence, 70
ineducability, 1, 21, 83
inferiority, 22, 48, 49, 55, 57, 67
initiative, 72, 139
innate ability, 2, 15, 61
intelligence, 2, 10, 15, 16, 19, 20, 34, 35, 66, 69, 70, 93, 103, 108, 127
   low, 9, 11, 12, 33, 35, 67, 68, 78, 84
   effect of emotional disturbance on, 14–16, 66, 109
intelligence quotient, 1, 5, 6, 10, 12, 14, 15, 16, 17, 21, 22, 24, 25, 34, 50, 66, 68, 69, 73, 78, 81, 96, 97, 103, 108
   changes in, 15, 16, 69–70, 78, 81–109
intelligence tests, 14
interests, 7, 84, 104, 115, 117, 126, 128, 139, 140, 141, 144
   expression of, 86–109

justice, 75, 77

leisure, 40–2, 143–4
limitations, 49, 77, 89

maladjustment, 16, 66–109
maturation, 70–2
meals, 57, 139
mental age, 15, 16, 61, 81, 96, 97, 103, 108, 119, 125, 127, 130, 134, 142–3
mental handicap in children, 47, 67, 110, 127, 129, 140, 143
   criteria for ascertainment, 3, 63, 141
   and delinquency, 33–46, 49
   and development, 12–17, 48, 53, 70–3, 83, 97
   and education, 2, 3, 5–12
   and parents' attitudes, 12–31, 48, 50
   and social training, 47–65, 118, 135–6, 140
misfits, 66–109
moral code, 6, 48

INDEX

moral code (contd.)
  responsibility, 38
  sentiments, 35
  standards, 6, 37, 74, 141
  suasion, 75
morals, 29, 41
music and mime, 73, 81, 97, 104, 106–8, 111, 117–18

neurosis, 66
number, 52, 80, 82, 87–9, 92, 94, 96, 102, 111, 128–39, 142
  and reading disability, 15, 125, 127, 142

occupation centre, 1, 3, 85

parents' attitudes, 18–32, 37, 48, 50, 71, 92, 98
parent-teacher association, 31–2
percussion, 106, 117
personality, 5, 7, 8, 9, 35, 47, 58, 68, 78, 80, 82, 101, 112, 118, 140
pets, 95–6, 113, 114
potentialities, 7, 10, 11, 21, 30, 47, 71, 81
privacy, 71, 73
project, 132, 139
probation, 40
psychiatric treatment, 66, 108
psychiatrist, 66, 70, 77, 82
psychoneuroses, 66
psychopathic tendencies, 66
punishment, 35, 74–77

reading, 10, 12, 52, 62, 64, 80, 92, 96, 102, 104, 106, 107, 111, 118–28, 142, 143
  activities, 121–4
  and number activity, 135–9
  books, 124
  comprehension, 116, 121, 123, 125
  disability, 15, 125, 127, 142
  emotional attitude, 127
  formal teaching, 121, 124–7
  and language, 118–20, 125

reading (contd.)
  mechanical, 120, 125
  pre-reading activities, 111, 118–24, 125, 126
  readiness, 119, 120
regression, 115, 141, 142
relationships, 47, 51, 53, 57, 80, 99, 114
  with family, 18–32, 48
  with moral code, 48
  with other children, 48, 72, 80
  with self, 48
  with society, 48
  with teacher, 50
remedial teaching, 16, 80
repetitive handwork, 115
resentment, 58, 74, 76, 77, 79
residential school, 34, 40, 58
responsibility, 35, 38, 56, 71, 72, 99, 141
rhythmic movement, 106, 117

security, 1, 28, 30, 48, 50, 51, 76, 77, 112
  lack of, 24, 28, 29, 79
segregation, 2, 6, 11, 67
self-confidence, 56
self-control, 6, 52, 62, 74, 112, 142
self-expression, 52, 53, 54, 113, 115, 118
self-realisation, 47, 49
self-reliance, 51, 60, 112, 141
self-respect, 6, 11, 55, 57, 133
sentiments, 35, 36, 47
service, 9, 52, 60
sex problems, 11, 40, 77, 78, 83–4
skills, 7, 110–36, 140, 143
social training, 47–65, 118, 135–6, 140
  adjustment, 76, 88–97, 99–109, 118
  conflict, 71
  contacts, 33, 82, 103
  co-operation, 53, 54, 63, 82, 107, 111, 139
  life, 2, 53, 71, 77, 80

social training (*contd.*)
  misfits, 66–109
  play, 49, 52, 71, 112
  relations, 47, 51, 53, 57, 80
society, 1, 5, 10, 11, 34, 47, 48, 49, 52, 54, 60, 61, 63, 80
solitude, 71, 72, 73, 79, 89, 99, 105
special educational treatment, 1, 140
special school
  activities, 52, 53, 57, 60, 63, 78
  activity methods, 51
  attitude of parents, 18–32, 37, 48, 50, 71, 92, 98
  buildings and equipment, 49, 90–1
  criteria for selection, 3, 12–17
  discipline, 58–9, 61
  misfits, 66–109
  social training, 47–65
  stigma, 2, 19
  teacher, 50–2
  transfer to secondary school, 127, 140

special school (*contd.*)
  treatment of delinquency, 33–46, 49, 67, 68, 74, 98, 103, 141
speech, 12–13, 53, 72–3, 81, 96, 105, 108, 118, 136
  teacher's, 119
  therapy, 73
stability, 10, 11, 24, 30, 36, 42, 47, 55, 57, 65, 78, 80, 112, 118, 140
statutory examination, 12, 13–14, 67, 69
sublimation, 61, 118
suggestibility, 33, 36
supervision, 11, 30, 36, 40, 42, 63, 68, 74, 110, 129, 142

time-table, 111
transfer to secondary school, 127
truancy, 29, 33, 34, 38, 40, 68, 74, 98–9, 102–3

withdrawal, 15, 49, 54, 57, 64, 73, 98–100, 103–9